International
Who's Who in Poetry

Judy Lynn
CHIEF EDITOR

INTERNATIONAL WHO'S WHO IN POETRY

Los Angeles, California

International Who's Who in Poetry (IV)

Library of Congress
Cataloging in Publication Data

ISBN 978-1-61936-068-6

Printed and manufactured in the United States of America by

International Who's Who in Poetry

Los Angeles, California

Foreword

Reality only reveals itself when it is illuminated by a ray of poetry.
–Georges Brague

We are so excited to welcome our published poets and appreciators of skilled expression to this beautiful collection of contemporary literary talent! As you traverse these bound pages, you will discover eclectic portrayals of life in well-crafted verse fit for interpretation, comprehension, identification and, above all, celebration. Throughout history and all cultures, the art of poetry has served to justify, nourish, develop, inform, imagine, portray and commemorate the human condition. Poetry has also always been pleasurable: both reading and composing verse is satisfying, comforting and cathartic. This is because in poetry, we find fragments of our own experiences, emotions and understandings. We also uncover opinions, strife, joy and wisdom foreign to our own, as a result of our maturity, practice or position in life. These revelations necessarily elevate our consciousness of others and develop greater sympathy and appreciation in us for people whose circumstances vary so much from our own that we tend to consider them beyond comprehension and relation. The commonality among humanity afforded by poetry, one too often alluded in daily life, makes this form of composition not only beautiful, but culturally righteous and sublime—as it provides a forum for crucial personal introspection and embodies the potential for colossal social advancement. Therefore, we are passionately devoted to presenting all kinds of poets, writing all kinds of poetry, and we hope you will devote some time to read and ruminate on the challenging, cultivating, tasteful and assorted work of these diverse artists. Take this opportunity to rejoice at your impressive accomplishments and read the array of unique creations featured within these pages. Remember how blessed we are to be moved to write, how grateful we should be to behold the art of others, and how wise we are to know the essential value in poetic expression.

Judy Lynn
Chief Editor

I Just Want to Be a Rock Star

I just want to be a rock star
but homework let's me down, down, down.
I just want to be a rock star
but homework let's me down, down, down.
I just want to
move it, move it, move it.
I just want to
do it ,do it, do it.
I just want to
prove it, prove it, prove it.
But homework let's me down.

Dasha Lukinova
Vernon Hills, IL United States

Eternity

Where will your journey take you?
From birth till death, we are on a journey to eternity.
This takes multiple choices for each of us.
Some are full of splendor and hope, while
Others are full of challenges.
Will you follow the way of Christ or
That of Satan, the deceiver?
The way of Christ is the true way, but
There will be trials and tribulations along the way.
Will your journey end with
An eternity with God in Heaven
Upon the acceptance of Christ that
Died on the Cross at Calvary for all our sins,
Or will your destination be an eternity
In Hell with your following of Satan
And rejection of Christ?
My final destination will be with
God the Father, the Son, and the Holy Spirit
In Heaven for all eternity.

Carla Waldrep
Gainesville, GA United States

Flights of Fancy

Dreams, birds of life,
Transporters.
Faith and hope elevated on their wings.

Thoughts, mind set free.
Cavorters.
Flit and fly unrestricted, far away.
Earthbound once more to fly another day.

Marilyn Russell
Belleir Bluffs, FL United States

The Locket

In her hand, she held a little locket—
Nothing gold about it, but for the memories it held
Of a child, whose picture was tucked inside.
As she gazed into his face,
There was a smile behind the tears,
Remembering another time and place.

Many times, she's held him—her pride and joy—
When he was just a boy,
And told him of lands far away.
She told him that he could be anything he dreamed,
And when he grew up, the world was his to see.
That was so long ago, it seemed.

Now his dreams had become reality;
He was traveling to the countries of the world.
And though she missed her little boy,
She was so proud of the young man he'd come to be.
His education and thirst for knowledge
Was taking him places that only few get to see.

Now looking once again at the little locket,
She brushes the tears from her eyes
And as she hooks the chain around her neck.
She says a prayer to God to keep him safe
And guide him on his way;
Then, she blows a kiss to the picture of his face.

Frances Atkinson Vaughn
Blanch, NC United States

I started writing poems and songs in high school. My senior year, I was voted class poet. Writing poetry was a way to express the feelings of my heart. All of my poetry has been about family, friends, and special times in my life. "The Locket" is one I wrote about my son while he was studying abroad in Europe. I was blessed to have another of my poems published earlier this year in another book. Thank you for giving me the opportunity to have one of my poems published and to share my poetry with others.

WWII

The sounds of liberation surrounds us, but still the stench of death
    astounds us
We hold our breaths with each sound of gunfire and bombs
With hope that freedom will befall us before the next one comes
They are filling the many tombs with our friends and next of kin
Two by two, we slowly march to our deaths
When will it end, must we proceed to die?
Will they ever come and free us so the rest can stay alive?

Viviana Diaz Casarez
Odessa, TX United States

I was born on March 4, 1989 in Odessa, TX and proudly graduated from Permian High School in 2007. I love to write and draw, and when I'm sure no one else besides my family is around, I love to sing. My family has told me I am very talented, and that is what inspired me to submit my poetry. My poetry and my drawings are my way of escaping reality and finding tranquility.

Light Through Lace

A giddy little feeling,
Gradually appealing,
Sneaks up on me in patterns warm
Like gentle light through lace.

Although it is alarming,
It's also truly charming!
I peek through and find I can't wipe
This smile from my face.

Who's to know if tomorrow
I'll find it all a sorrow?
But still today, I'll take a chance
At hoping, just in case.

And maybe, oh just maybe,
I'll be the lucky lady.
For after all, is it so long a shot
With help from grace?

Rebecca Loomis
Atchison, KS United States

Gone Fishin'

If you ask me what I did today
And all I do is gloat
You'll know I was out fishin'
On a big lake with my boat

Hooked my boat up to my truck
Grabbed some smokes, some bud and bait

Got up before dawn and fished all day long
And didn't come back till late

Got burnt to a crisp
Caught plenty of fish
Too tired to stand or to eat

I guess you can say I had a great day
But right now, I am totally beat

Best part of my story
Is this one day of glory
Helped me win a new rod and a reel

If you're not a bass master fisherman
You would say this is no big deal

We're a special breed of people
Proud of what we've achieved

The scrapbooks and trophies and that fish on the wall
And the look on our faces—it sure tells it all!

Barbara Wojtan
Clermont, FL United States

Capistrano

Pairing swallows wheel
in soaring exultation
of their bond,
a gossamer apart.
Dancing, dreaming, caring,
we exceeded them their flight.

Now, the swallows fly
and leave no ripples
in the sky—
only the wind,
to dry my welling eyes
and drown my stifled cry.

Robert Thompson
Vista, CA United States

I am a dual U.S. and Canadian citizen, who was born at the start of WWII. I am a free spirit and have traveled and lived in Hawaii, New Zealand, Australia, Singapore, Teheran, Delhi, Cairo, Athens, Venice, Milan, Paris, London, Montreal, Boston, New York, D.C., Edmonton, Spokane, Seattle, Vancouver, Monterey and San Diego. I love Life, nature and helping people. Every day is the first day of the rest of my life.

A Goodnight Kiss

Oh! How I wish I could
Give her, but one goodnight kiss
Affection shown from my heart to hers
As she drifts off into a slumbering bliss

I could see laying but a gentle kiss
Upon her soft, angelic cheek
And whisper to her, "Goodnight love…
I'll await you in my dreams."

A kiss from lips as soft
As the pillow where lies her head
Such relaxation for her that she had never felt before
That she lays her head on my chest and in my arms instead

Her ear pressed along my chest
To get the mere chance to listen to my heartbeat
Like a lullaby, music to her ears
As she drifts slowly off to sleep

As I cherish the privilege
Of watching her sleep
I think to myself, "God…
I don't deserve this blessing of having this angel of yours next to me."

"Lord, I couldn't thank you enough.
There really are no words.
I can't help, but to always wonder…
am I really worthy of her?"

Through all of her frights and fears
Her smiles and her tears
That when awakens from them all,
She knows that I am there

As she opens those eyes
To the blessing of another sunrise
I can't help but look at this stunningly beautiful woman and say,
"Blessed is the man that wakes up by her side."

With bright light of her eyes
Glaring from that very somber sunrise
Is the most majestic image of God's creation
Enough to make a man cry

Cry out tears of joy, happiness
Cries of thanks unto the Lord
For the blessing of this angel, here on earth
The best blessing, I never deserved

You would never have thought
The intimacy from a goodnight kiss meant so much
What it means to have our lips draw us closer
By just allowing them one last touch

Such love from a single kiss
By God, might it be made to last
Oh, but to lay but one single kiss upon her cheek
Even if it is to be but my last.

Kenneth Davis
Dyer, TN United States

Family Literacy in USA

For many years, I have wanted to be a teacher
What type of teacher?
I have bachelors of science in mathematics
Do I have any politics?
I did not expect to be an ESL tutor.
I try to make the class not a bore
I am volunteering, because I want more literate families
Hopefully, finding a job should be more of an ease
I do not want people in jail, if not necessary
Any wholesome job is good, even if, temporary
I enjoy my students' companionships
It has not been just student and teacher relationships
Some of the students have brought their culture's food
My boredom at home has changed to an exploratory mood
I am glad and not sad about this decision
I do my best when it comes to basic English precision
I hope I am helping others to stay away from criminal activities
I hope my students have homes and do use keys
I hope I am teaching others how to communicate better
I hope my students have homes and are settlers
I hope I am informing them with useful sentences
I hope my students listen to my good intention dispenses

Yee-Ling Chau
Sugarland, TX United States

A Diamond in the Rough

Just as the sun illuminates the world from above
And the oceans waves hug the shores with its love,
The air's ability to give breath to life,
A blessed gift from heaven—the earth, its wife.

Soon arrives the presence of the mysterious night,
A time of sleep with the moon to sparkle so bright.
For the secrets within the earth the darkness shall keep,
To uncover that diamond in the rough that will cause a woman to
    weep.

Just as the sun, she brightens up his world,
And with so much love he proposes to his girl.
Together, they two, will be able to give breath to a new life,
The most blessed gift of a son for a husband and a wife.

Soon will come the end to the rest of their lives,
A time for eternal rest with no more pain and no more cries.
For the secret they have found was the life they spent as one,
The diamond that started it all has now been passed down to their son.

Anthony Demapan
Corona, CA United States

*I was mainly inspired by few promising and everlasting relationships that are so
hard to find now these days. This poem is more of a reminiscing future for me,
which I hope to have. The diamond ring was more personal, because my mother
had given hers to me; I plan to it keep forever, as it holds as great amount of
sentimental value to me. Remember; "If the love is true, then the life is real."—
Anthony Demapan*

The Bills

I am not unlike our nation—
I have cash flow constipation
And great intimidation,
From the daily debt inflation of my bills.

Yes the bills, bills, bills, bills, bills, bills, bills, bills
Have become a constellation,
And I need emancipation
From the constant procreation of the bills.

I have stress and consternation,
It's a fear I can't ignore.
Now I resort to automation,
To keep collectors from my door.

I have great anticipation
of the eventual dissipation of my bills.
And I never send to know for whom the bills are totaled,
They've been totaled up for me.

Auto bill-pay helps me pay them,
And keeps the debt threats far away.
Though there is now less fear and mayhem,
I eat smaller meals each day.

So I will pay the bills, bills, bills, bills, bills, bills, bills—
I'll pay the damn bills until I go bats or I'm bill free!

John Vizzuto
Vincent, OH United States

My Prayer

I cry in silence, so no one hears,
Except you, my God—you know my fears.
Trying not to think of the whats or ifs,
I pray to you, the pain moves swift.
The sadness I have from my broken heart—
How heavy it is, too heavy to cart.
Lift up my heart so I can move on;
Adjust my focus, I need to be strong.
My grief is endless—the one whom I lost,
I wanted him to stay, no matter the cost.
Was I so selfish to ask of this,
As I tenderly gave him my very last kiss?
My heart was not whole from that time on,
As my beloved is not here; he has gone.
Remove this sorrow, I wish not to keep.
Leave me happy memories I may dream in sleep.
So touch my heart relieve this pain—
Give me a promise I will see him again.

Lynette Nash
Muswellbrook, NSW Australia

I live in a country town in Australia. I work hard and don't have a lot of time to write as much as I would like. I often take time to look inside of myself, to see if I have become the person I need to be; this I express in my writing and art. The things that are important to me are family and friends—these make me complete. This poem is about my father, who now has been taken in death. He was my best friend. I hope I am the person he will always be proud of, and my wish is to one day see him again.

Encore

I walk on the stage acting so brave;
my heart can't even take it.

Assata McLeod
Charlotte, NC United States

I started writing at the age of eight, then I went onto writing more. The whole reason I started to write was because I loved it. I realized I had a talent in writing and I can write about how I am feeling, when I am feeling up to it. The most important thing is the feeling to me and how I write it.

Fear

day by day
year by year.
we live in constant fear
fear of what the seasons may hold
are fear that our economy may fold.
fear from the actions we take
or fear of not knowing our fate
our fear may come from sights and sounds
it may also come from our leaps and bounds
but fear is something we all need around
for it goes a long way to keep us sound
if one did not have any fear
the heart would not be as dear.

Dale Andrews
Farmingdale, NJ United States

Ponder

Life's progression, from birth
To one's final conclusion,
Is marked by change and
heartbreak;

We run the gamut of life's
Calendar, trying always
To adapt to the strong
Currents of existence.

Our encounters with human
Confusion gives us both
Challenge and calm and
Tears with smiles.

It's remarkable we manage
To survive, but we do;
And all the while, we
Take each moment and life.

Richard Huggins
Lakeland, FL United States

Reminiscing Once Again

Here I go again with memories of yore
while I listen to the oldies of long ago—
"My Memories of You" takes me back
to the eighth grade, a shy teen was I then.

And "A Casual Look" reminds me of my
sweet high school days, as well as
that old fort-five by Elvis, "I Was The One."
And who could forget slow dancing to
"There's A Moon Out Tonight"? For
it reminds me of my future husband
being shipped overseas.

Where were you when "A Thousand Miles Away"
or "Sincerely" was played on the radio,
or "My Dearest Darling" or
"Over The Mountain" by Johnnie and Joe?
And remember "Earth Angel," or "One Summer Night,"
and slow-dancing over and over to
"What's Your Name?"

These nostalgic memories, they conjure up
a carefree life and a happy teen—
making the most of her young life
and making the teenage scene.

Alicia Griego
San Antonio, TX United States

Night Wind, to Eve

Why do you grasp... so desperately?
When your heart flutters,
Like a fallen leaf
To the visit of a warm, night wind
That you cannot see,
but only feel...
As memories among hidden dreams
That rustle to the whisper of distant trees

A promise...
Another journey from yourself
To awaken again in another's eyes
Who you think you see, but only know
As a silhouettes...
And backlit images of what you lack
That ride on whispers in the night wind.

So you flutter
And forget who feels that beating heart—
Fighting those tears about to swell
As night waves to take you,
up and down...
A surfer under starlit skies,
To the endless diamond beach in your heart

Peeter Lamp
New York, NY United States

I write only when the muse moves me, not for the sake of making poems. When she will come is a mystery, but when present, my pen is set on fire, and the words burn until the flames are exhausted. All the originals are by hand, for a keyboard deadens the flames. But once done, the keyboard becomes quite handy and the printouts I visit daily—listening for whatever calls for change, until the poem becomes quiet as a calm lake. Then it has found its form. For the record, I live in New York City.

A Heart Betrayed

Lust, violent passion, heat the summer night
Love's begging plea a heart betrayed love's
One and only plight
Longing fear, longing hate, longing tears fall
Quietly in the summer rain
Pain and passion become one in the same
The heart's one and only mistake
Anger, rage, retching screams
Loves passion love's tenderness, a long-lost dream
To feel again, to love again a wish of
The heart put asunder
The heart, longing, will have no other
Wanting, loving, shriek of agony
Pain has surfaced to nothing but shame
Wanting powerful tearing love like a
Pounding, screeching, powerful retching
Rain
I know now that my heart will never
Survive a heart betrayed
It will never ever be the same

Carmon Brown
Omaha, NE United States

Panda Bear

Don't be afraid dear Panda Bear
Of your heart—for it to run, fly, or be shared.
Your emotions were once held tight in a snare
I freed you; you wondered why, dear Panda Bear.

I wanted to be your soul mate,
Your heart was once filled with hate.
I took it away, as you began to bawl
I caught you as you began to fall.

Don't cry, dear Panda Bear
I am here for you—
To give you a heart, as good as new
To fall in love with my dear Panda Bear.

I mended your broken heart
Filled it with kindness, a beautiful piece of art
Knowing that from your side, I will never depart
From the Panda Bear with a mended heart.

"I love you," says the Panda Bear.
My dear Panda Bear, I will always love you and care.

Elizabeth Pedroza
Blythe, CA United States

"Panda Bear" is dedicated to my special someone in life, my dear Panda Bear. My thanks go to my family and of course, my Panda Bear, for always being proud of and encouraging my writing.

L.U.S.T.

Living by the laws of the heart with

Unpurified thoughts running wild

Sweet desires that cloud the mind

True love is but only the delusion.

Gretchen Piper
Colorado Springs, CO United States

Hope

Struggling to find a place in this world and where I belong
I walk this pathway alone, not caring which way is wrong
No matter what happens, no matter how long
No matter what, I will always be strong

I will always believe in hope forever
You can make me lose my hope never
No matter what or how clever
You can't catch me, ever

Reina Ly
Kingsland, GA United States

I am twelve. I was born on December 16, 1999, and I started to write poems when I was little, regardless of whether or not they were good. I write poems based on how I feel, like when I am mad or sad or happy. Sometimes when I feel really bad, I write about hope and staying strong. I want my poems to speak to the reader and hope they understand and encourage them to express their feelings. Everyone says I am amazing at writing poems, but the thing is I just found a special talent to express my feelings, and I am not the only one. I also hope my poems can be lessons to some of you. I love poetry so much, and bottom line is my poems mean the world to me. It is a part of me and who I am, and I am glad to share it with you. I hope you enjoy.

Waters of Redemption

When first we met, your smile said, "Come to me, we will tread the
waters together—
Cool and gentle splashing against our skin." Attention we didn't pay;
we stood mesmerized in each other's arms
A flash of lighting, a bolt of thunder, turbulence turned the waters
dark. We were lost, drifting aimlessly apart. We cried out, but neither
could hear
Years flew by; we went our own ways, only to remember the days of the
cool calm of the waters
Chance meetings in far places—a glance, a smile, lunch, casual
conversation, gazed into each other's eyes, kissed holding each other
tight, turned and walked away
Spring turned to summer, summer to fall, fall to winter
With age in our eye's and gray in our hair, by chance we met and
crossed the crystal sea and tread the waters of redemption
Together in loving arms we will always be, you and me

Roberta Johnson
Albia, IA United States

Fool Playing a Fool

Playing love games with you, I really played a fool
Say it ain't true falling for the lies from you
The childish b*llsh*t won't take precedence
You're in a league of your own, turning cheek to cheek
Never looking back 'cause the fool you played you thought was me

Step in the ring, baby
The champ is here to stay
Playing love games with this fool isn't quite the same
You say you have it all figured out
Well, baby, let's see the destined play for play

Emotions are known to take over me
Playing with this fool never could be believed
See the mind is everything you need it to be
Tired, fixed, and a bit of a mess
No doubt, truly, I can say I am blessed

You didn't see this coming
A fool playing a fool is never intrigued
It is an opposite emotion, cold in disbelief
You see when you look in the mirror, the fool you played was me!

Kresha Gipson
Santa Fe Springs, CA United States

When Moms Die

When moms die, they leave behind
so many people of so many kinds.

One thing they all share is the love of one life
who, without all her love and struggles and strife,
would not be here today or tomorrow
to share in their joys or even sorrows.

They look to the future, it looks so bare...
Remember, her memories will always be there.

She made some mistakes...
Haven't we all?
Sometimes she'd stumble,
or even fall.

Toward the end of her life, her body did fail...
it made the good times they had grow pale.

But one thing's for sure
in God's plan of life:
without our moms,
we wouldn't have life!

So, miss her, we will...remember her fondly,
treasure the good times, let go of the bad...
Know that God sent her for the plans He had.

Carol Fross
Tampa, FL United States

L.O.V.E.

It is never unjust or slightly one-sided
It is tranquil and soft, never close-minded
It is slow and steady; rain on a window pane
It is blunt and decisive, sometimes quite plain

It will never cause strife or vast friction
It is never predictable or frequent in diction
It is strong and wise, an eagle to be in time
It is never envious, vain or forever unkind

It is never arrogant or eternally estranged
It is always free and evermore unchained
It is food for the soul that does not give way
It is patiently there, and there it will stay

Erika Rivera
Milwaukee, WI United States

Everyone always has that one dream they stand by and mine is poetry. My family comes from little money, but we manage well. I am just happy to know my dream will finally be noticed by others. I will continue to write poetry in the years to come.

One Wish

If I could make one wish…
It would be to know everything.

To know every thought
Every desire
Every fantasy
Every favorite thing
Every fear that your mind harbors

If I could have one wish…
It would be to make you real.

To dwell on every thought
Fulfill every desire
Make every fantasy come true
Observe every favorite thing
Fight away every fear that haunts you

If I could have one wish…
It would be to make me real to you.

To feel every touch
To hear every thought said
To grant you everything I could

Now tell me…
What would your wish be?

Elisa Laycock
Greencastle, IN United States

A Steady Beat

You have a heart with a steady beat
A simple melody without any notes
A heart with many meanings of
Life, love and heartbreak
Without a heart we cannot live
And a heart that's shattered
Makes us not want to live
A heart's tempo quickens
As love crosses our path
A heart's beating loud as a bass drum
Or as quiet as a metronome
What locks up our heart
That blinds our view
From our rights and wrongs
Both love and hate blocks our view
Like foggy glass on a window's pane
A broken heart is not something
That can be physically done
Like a fractured arm
Or a heart attack
Even so, we feel the pain
With every heartbeat
With every beating pulse
With every "broken heart"

Paris Nguyen
Garden Grove, CA United States

Nocturnal Thoughts

The world has become so corrupt from evil that human life isn't valued as highly anymore—wickedness and death seem to mock all effort to find purpose in life. Since life on earth has no meaning to some people, it should be enjoyed by others; but how can we enjoy life, when we emphasize the universality of death more than we do living? What a pity for us not to
care about a life we didn't create, a life that was specially crafted and specifically designed for each individual. Remember: we were fearfully and wonderfully made. Every decision we make leads us down a different road or path; this is what makes us distinguishing. These unique decisions lead us on a new, profound discovery, journey, and adventure. Every decision that we make has significance, no matter the size—that's why humans are so distinctive in form, because we were made in superior quality by a superior creator, God.

Kayla Deshawn Servick
Emeryville, CA United States

I was born in Oakland, CA. I go to school at Patten Academy, and I love writing poetry. I love writing poetry because it releases stress, and you can express your feelings creatively. Poetic power is amazing—it's uplifting, and its inspirational. You can open a whole new world with poetry, so don't be afraid to explore the creativity of the mind, travel outside your mental boundaries and expand your imagination—go beyond your limits. Feed your mind with enthusiasm, immerse yourself in your wildest fantasies, because your thoughts or words are so valuable.

Untitled

Why did you not let me die?
A simple dose of Cyanide,
Your life would have simply stopped,
With the final toll of the eternal clock.

Your life would have ended, the pain inside,
The lives of your loved ones would have been fine.
Now all you need is a blade across your wrist,
One more death, added to his long list.

The young girl would suddenly scream,
As the gunshot ripped her heart free.
The reaper of night would take her hand
And add her soul to his marching band.

The young male stepped across the street—
The truck took his life, without missing a beat.
One more soul, one more death.
The reaper laughed, with a single breath.

Michael T. Henderson
Port Huron, MI United States

The Love of My Life

The first time we met, I knew I would fall in love—
it's like he was sent to me from above.
In the beginning, it was great; we had a lot of fun.
Before I knew it, I was in love. He was my number one.
He would always know what to say and do to make me feel so good;
but after a while, things changed like I knew it would
I didn't know it at the time,
but he was slowly corrupting my mind.
It really is true when people say love is blind.
He made me feel hopeless: no hopes, no dreams
But I can't live without him, it seems
I was miserable when he wasn't with me
he's turning me into someone I don't wanna be
He wanted me all for himself, he didn't want to share
My family hated him, but I really don't care
No matter how bad he treats me, I had to be with him everyday
I cant live without you, no matter what you do or say
I was always tough, I would never take any sh*t
but I let him beat me every day—hit after hit
One day I will be strong enough to go
You will soon be someone I used to know
Getting over this man is the hardest thing I will ever do
because this man isn't a man at all...who knew?
This man is my drug addiction;
but, trust me, all I have said is far from fiction
I had to have him every day, I loved him very much
but he messed up my life forever with just one touch
I can't ever say I finally beat him but I have him under control
I will always miss him but will never go back to that dark hole
Yes the love of my life is a drug,
but don't judge me—because anyone can get bitten by the love bug

Erin Tavares
Fall River, MA United States

I battled with a drug addiction for a long time. No matter how horrible the things I did were, my family and boyfriend of seven years stood by my side and never gave up on me—even when I gave up on myself. I decided to submit "The Love of My Life," because it's very important to me for people to have a better understanding about addiction and how it takes over your life. Addicts choose to start taking drugs, but they don't have the privilege to have the choice to stop. I always enjoyed writing poems for personal view. I submitted this poem without any expectations, and I'm honored to have this opportunity. I thank everyone who enjoyed my poem.

How?

How can I feel
So much pain inside
So much hurt, regret, and resent,
When I look out my window-
my dirty, limiting window-
and see the same?
How can I feel so sorry for myself
When someone out there-
Someone beyond which my eye can see-
Feels the same sorrow in their heart?
How can you feel so much
Then listen to the songbirds and hear it repeated
In a melody that brings tears to your eyes?
You can smell it in the air
In the way the roses wither
And the sorry sound of a rusty train
Far off in the distance.
Before you complain
About whatever ails you
Hold in your tears
Save them in your heart
And when you really need them
Let them go.

Mary Kasputis
Herndon, VA United States

My friends, family, and teachers make me who I am. I'm sarcastic, athletic, and I love to have fun. I've always loved words and how they can be strung together almost musically to share emotion. I write what I feel. "Discovery isn't seeing what no one else has seen, but thinking what no one else has thought."

Firefighters

While others were fleeing out
They went boldly in.
Up they went, disdaining doubt
If one life they might win.

Rumors of lives at dire risk
Spurred them up and on.
343 would join the list
of those who would not see dawn.

Greater love had none than those
Who gave their final breath
As they in mortal peril chose
To save another life from death.

Those martyrs were Christ-like in this
They gave their lives for strangers.
May they all be now in heavenly bliss
With the One who came in a manger.

The moral here that we must learn
My sisters and my brothers
Is to help us our self-interest spurn
And give ourselves for others.

George Guntermann
Salem, OR United States

George Guntermann has written devotional poetry for more than twenty years. His poetry reflects his profound love for God and for all people. He lives in Salem, OR and serves at Salem House of Prayer, a local service ministry.

The Geek

In my eyes, individuality makes me unique;
But in your eyes, it makes me a geek.
All the things I've faced—you couldn't imagine.
I wanna forget, give up, or give in.
I'm falling apart, getting ready to crack...
I'm just a shade in the dark, fading to black.
Then I see the light, and it's pulling me through.
And I realize: why should I care about you?
You don't give my the time of day
Or listen to what I say.
So here I lay...
don't worry, I'm okay.
Actually, I am better than ever! Without an ounce of regret!
The things I have been through I will never forget.
They've made me stronger, I'm no longer weak—
But deep down within me, somewhere, lies the geek.

Jane Sagoe
Hagerstown, MD United States

I started writing poetry when I was eight years old. I really just did it for fun. I am now thirteen. This is my very first serious poem. I decided to write it when I got the email about this opportunity, and I wanted my second published poem to really move people. I wanted people out there who are struggling to know life does get better. This poem is loosely based on bullying and for kids my age, but I feel like people of all ages could relate to it. I personally am a very happy person, but I just wanted to be serious for once, and I hope this poem moves someone out there. I don't care how many—even if I can make a difference in just one person's life, it would be worth it.

My Little Blue Jacket

In my little blue jacket, there I see
You smiling with your friends so casually.
I can't help but watch you, can't help but stare—
Can't help but wishing I was over there.

You look my way, and I avert my eyes;
I'm scared of what you'd say to the guys.
I look up again, to see you staring...
In my direction, not caring.

I look in your eyes and I blush.
How pathetic am I to gush?
Now then, you blink and turn your head;
I guess you weren't looking at me, I dread.

My heart sinks, it was all too good,
You to look at me? Like you ever would.
I sink and I sigh, so saddened by grief.
When the bell rings, I'm happy to leave.

The next morning comes, and I see you,
You come in with jacket, all stylish and new.
But secretly I hoped you'd notice me—
But I guess you really can't change society.

Kristina Hutto
Cypress, TX United States

I am only a soul who loves to write. I'm thankful for my family and friends; I don't think I could do it without them. I'm so elated and honored to be published in this book! I love poetry and writing, and I don't think I'll ever stop. Though the era of reading from a classic book is falling, I'll always be in love with turning the page and becoming one with the story.

Beautiful

Molested and tested as a young child
I was destined to survive and strive for the best
inside I felt I was a mess
because I couldn't understand what it was to be blessed
my faith many times pushed beyond belief
I never felt I'd come under from beneath
from beneath continued mental, physical, and sexual abuse
from beneath my depression and low self-esteem
feeling like my beauty and presence meant I was a worthless little thing
people in general tried to destroy me—I hid, I ran, I cried, and
    everything
but one day while in my closet feeling broken, dirty
used and alone, I heard a gentle whisper, felt a security
a hug from unfamiliar arms; it was God, and He spoke to me
I do love you and always have, you are beautiful—even torn
it's what I made you to be
you're one of My strongest creations
and I knew if any, My child, you'd rise above and succeed
these obstacles were merely the power I saw you'd need to have the
    wisdom
and strength to accomplish your greatest dreams

Monika Russell
San Antonio, TX United States

Through My Eyes

I see beautiful colours through my eyes
I feel beautiful colours from the skies
I hear wonderful sounds through my eyes
This is truth, I tell no lies
I may be different, yet still the same
I may be a wonder, yet I am sane
Come to my world for just a day
I'll show you magic in my own way
I may fear from time to time
Yet through my eyes, my world is fine
Autism, there's no need for cries
My life is wonderful through my eyes.

Monique Smith-Carroll
Oakliegh South, Victoria Australia

My poetry comes from within, experiences I have had in life and all that surrounds me.

Black, Iced, and Tall

She walks into the caf
All eyes are on her as her body sways
She brings the heat on the hottest day
The night before lingers like a sore
Smudged mascara, clogged pores
But all are speechless as they huddle closer
To hear her order without a flaw
Black, iced, and tall
Heels high, skirt small, vanilla skin
And maybe just a little bit of sugar
She adds, leaning in, letting her Venti cups show
Cinnamon spice grin, all the boys take it in
Like they just had a double shot of espresso
Twirling her mocha hair into a bun, she says, thanks hon
With a wink to the barista, he is frappe' in her hands
She adds her own cream
Her order is complete, so she heads for the street
She catches a stare of one boy who seems uncharmed
She's as predictable as a tall, skim, caramel macchiato
Her artificially sweetened heart skips a beat
He knows, oh he knows

Hope Braley
Allston, MA United States

I'm a student studying music therapy at Berklee College of music, but my first passion has always been writing. I write short stories, poetry, and I am currently working on a book. I feel compelled to write what is honest and true, even if it's not pretty. It's important to me to always be reading and learning about new things so I can grow as an individual. I enjoy spending time with my friends, traveling, and being outdoors. I love living in Boston right now, but I hope to one day live in California or England, working as a music therapist and continue writing about life and all its little quirks. Cheers!

Strip

Poetry makes me trip,
It makes me want to strip
And make love to the world
Until the sun is out.
Undress all the lies,
The shame and falsehood.
Turn my back to the hypocrite,
Tweet to the universe
That this is what poetry is all about.
From the top of my lungs,
Scream out loud:
I am not afraid anymore,
As I recite from a cloud.
Words fly all around me,
Like mystic butterflies.
Open arms, open eyes...
Yes, I am free.

Flavia Rocha Loures
Washington, DC United States

Flavia Rocha Loures is an environmental attorney, working since 2005 at WWF, in Washington, D.C. Her first poetry book compiles the poems she wrote over the last twenty years, depicting the various stages of her life in rhymes.

Cuba Is a Lonely Island

I think back about the nights
we almost loved each other to death.
How lonely I felt living with you—
More lonely than the moon floating in space.

Dried roses hang upside down, caressing the walls;
A cemetery of Love. You bring me bloodless, blue roses.
I'm dying with you.

Like my beloved Cuba,
An abandoned beauty,
Decaying, black, molded walls,
smeared red lipstick,
Our fluids become One.

I too feel empty and bruised.
My heart filled with cracks that reflect the light of a thousand colors.

Lonely like a Cuban refugee.
Lonely like a Cuban dictator,
Imprisoned like his son.
Cuba is a lonely island,
A lonely island like me.
But it was in Cuba where I learned to be free.

Maria Figueredo
New York, NY United States

Maria Angelica was born in Manhattan's Lower East Side and grew up in Hell's Kitchen and Riverdale. She is from Cuban-Greek descent. She studied at the School of American Ballet and danced in The Nutcracker at the age of eleven for the New York State Theatre in Lincoln Center. When she was twelve, thirteen and fourteen, she won first place in her school's declamation/monologue contest. The first one she did was from Tennessee Williams' This Property Is Condemned. Maria graduated from high school six months early and traveled along the East Coast with an improvisational theater company. She continued studying drama at NYU, Tisch School of the Arts and spent a year abroad in a New York/Paris student exchange program, where she completed an acting apprenticeship with the Theater of the Oppressed, directed by the late Augusto Boal. Maria modeled in New York city and in Italy and appeared in several music videos, all the while volunteering in soup kitchens, homeless shelters and reading for underprivileged children in schools. (One of her visions is to be involved in charities on a global spectrum.) Maria's work includes theatre, commercials, television and film. She appeared in a cameo role on the TV show, Rescue Me, playing opposite Denis Leary. She was also in a short film, The Bronx Balletomane (which won several awards), playing opposite Federico Castelluccio. In November 2012, she will start working in another film, directed by Tommy Clohessy. Maria has written a screenplay based on true events from her life in New York City and Cuba. She will play one of the leads and co-produce the project. This poem was written specifically for this film. "The first poem I ever wrote, at the age of eight, was a love poem to my mother. She always encouraged me to continue writing but since she was my mother, I thought it was just a sweet biased opinion and didn't listen. I never thought they were good enough. But I kept on writing for myself. I showed my writing to other people and again got great feedback. I just got lucky again, I thought, so instead I focused on other artistic endeavors."—Maria Angelica

Violent Streets

We walk down the streets
In a strange and distant land
With fear in our hearts
And weapons in hand

Locked and loaded
Alert at all times
Watch out for your partner
Leave no man behind

Be true to yourself
And what you believe
We're all here for one reason
As far as I can see

They've chosen the best
To find this one man
So check all gear
We're on our way to Afghanistan

I regret to say
We lost sergeant Pete
It happened so fast
Walking down those violent streets.

Kenneth Combs
Pahrump, NV United States

I am so honored to have my work noticed. I write a lot about the things going on inside our military; that is what inspires me the most. I was in the military, but was injured while serving. Now I'm a disabled veteran. All I can say is God is great; He gave me the gift of writing. He took the weapons from my hands and replaced them with a pen and paper. I could not be more content. I love this gift, and I will continue to honor those brave young men and women of our military with my writings.

One Day to Dullas

Emotionless, I watched you leave—
My insides knotting, wanting to scream.
I held back my tears, my sobs, my sorrow
And quietly wondered: how will I make it to tomorrow?
You see, you lightened a flame that had never been lit;
Holding me tight, we were the perfect fit.
Both of us knowing we felt more than lust.
Dropping my walls, I gave you my trust.
A trust I have given none other before,
I now find myself in turmoil on the floor.
Missing your touch, your comfort, your kiss,
And wondering when again I shall feel such bliss.
The strength of your arms, the warmth of your chest,
The thrill of your tongue massaging my neck.
So, I will cherish these memories and hold them all dear—
And hope that someday, again you'll be here.

Violet Adjei
Washington, DC United States

The Doorway

It is but a doorway,
A path to further life.
The transition from one to the other is brief—
A gentle rest, as of sleep,
Deeper and sounder in solitude.

Yet, you are not alone:
Others have come before, others will come after.
Your footsteps tread a well-worn path
Where other's feet have stepped.

The passage of time only smooths the path;
It does not erase, nor can it.
Life is a little space of time,
The moving of small clock hands
Which measure that part of time, until
The spring unwound—it stops.

But the well-spring of life, the soul itself
Moves on, lives on, apart and free!
Death with feather footsteps comes
To hold with gentle touch your soul.

It is but a doorway,
And we step through…

Michael Phifer
Naperville, IL United States

Michael is a retired ERP project manager who's been writing poetry for over fifty years. Michael has an MA in US colonial history and a double major in English and history. He is also the owner of the largest signed collection of non-sports trading cards in the world. He enjoys bowling, writing and meeting with his friends in the comic book and fantasy art industries.

Love Me Now

If you`re ever going to love me
love me now so I can know
All the sweet and tender words
from which real affection flow.

Love me now while I am living
do not wait till I am gone.
And then chisel it in marble
warm love words on ice cold stone.

If you've dear sweet words about me
why not whisper them to me.
Don't you know that it would make
me just as happy as happy can be?

If you wait till I am sleeping
never to waken here again,
there would be a wall between us
and I could not hear you then.

So dear,if you love me any at all
even if it's just a little bit
Love me now while I am living
so that I can own and treasure it.

Arlena Cox
Akron, NY United States

Rebellion

Fate has been wrapped around his finger,
Since before he could remember.
The bindings are too tight;
It's turning to the colour of night.
That finger will fall off one of these days,
But it won't phase him.
He is on a mission,
One full of passion.
Shivers plague his spine—
All he can taste is brine.
He will push on,
Even when they are gone.
Being pushed in the one direction his whole life
Has led him to abandon even his wife.
Too many funerals he has attended,
Too many to comprehend.
It's all he has ever known,
The seeking of the throne.
Since before he could remember,
Fate has been wrapped around his finger.

Andrew Hyde
Guelph, ON Canada

Tranquility

Oh stars, how beautiful you shine
Unable to be measured
Despite how we strive
You gaze down with such
Tranquility at night
That ever I wonder
Whene'er you're in sight
Such mindless beauty
Such ceaseless delight
My heart is enraptured
My mind ceases flight
No matter my comfort
No matter my strife
When you gaze down at me
All's well in my life
I look up at you
To cease all my fright
To soften my heart
And open my eyes
For when I gaze up at you
Jesus sends me His love
And my heart is transported
To the One up above

Shannon McCarville
Chester, AR United States

Goodbye

I thought you told the truth
but you just told me lies
I see the answer now when
I look into your eyes

I thought you loved me
I guess I was wrong
It was too good
to last for so long

The time has come
please don't cry
I have to do this
now I must say goodbye.

Tanya Anderson
Williston, ND United States

I started writing as a young girl just to express my feelings—as though it was my little journal of free expressions. As I wrote more poems, the more I enjoyed writing. A lot of my poems are from life experiences, and it's been a healing process as well. I grew up in a small town and knew I wouldn't get noticed, but accepted that. Yet at thirty-four, I am still expressing life experiences through my poetry.

I Want to Run

I want to run as fast I can, but I do not know to where—
Could be to nowhere, or to another far place,
Since I do not know what I will find there.

Even though I do not know what I will do when I find it,
I have been given 86,400 seconds of life each day. And life
Is the only game that comes without instructions:
How do I will play it?

I could have to be someone or I could become nothing.
Something I will find there—the only thing that I want to find
Is peace.
Will be there?

Simon Marcus
Carrollton, TX United States

I'm an ordinary human person who, every morning when I wake up, prays to God and gives Him thanks to be alive and the opportunity to live this day—and the additional days he is willing to give me. I live day by day under uncertainty regarding what challenges I will confront. Will there be the opportunity to go on? What will I find? I hope mainly for peace to all mankind, and health and luck in finding what I'm looking for. My poetry reflects this thinking.

Whispering Stranger

You awaken without opening your eyes,
Hearing becomes your first sense to be aroused.
There is a whispering you do not recognize—
Has some stranger invaded your domain?
You listen closer to bring about some recognition;
The sound is not human nor animal,
Nor the sounds of the traffic,
Or any other sound of the city.
Then your thoughts begin to gather,
And the trip you made becomes clearer.
With the sounds and sights of civilization,
You have tried to separate yourself and your senses.
You needed a break—time to relax and regroup—
So with a few necessities you left the city,
Starting a journey you have longed to take,
Into the mountains among the wilderness.
Upon opening your eyes you stare through the mist,
Rising above the trees is a sight you have not often witnessed—
The sun, without a halo of smog, clear and bright.
And again you close your eyes and just enjoy,
The whisper of the wind.

Roger Wilson
Flint, MI United States

I am a retired factory worker who enjoys writing and traveling. Since taking up putting thoughts on paper, I find a joy in letting others read perhaps a new perspective on life.

Why Play Games?

Relationships are like the game Battleship—
sometimes you hit, others you miss.
Baby, you sunk me
with your smile that is so lovely.
I lost the game, but won you;
let's keep playing, just us two.
We aren't drawing a card in Candy Land,
but playing poker knowing we have the best hand.
It's not having the most money in Monopoly,
it's about making never-ending memories.
We aren't rolling the dice in Yahtzee—
happily ever after is all that I see.
Let's not plan our moves like Chess;
all I know is a future with you would be the best.
I'm not trying to conquer your heart like Risk,
I want to sweep you off your feet with a kiss.
We don't have to put the pieces together like Scrabble,
in the name of love what we get to dabble.
You should know you can find love in me, don't guess Professor Plum.
Your heart isn't a game, so I won't play it like one.

Zane Price
Aurora, CO United States

Love is the greatest gift in the world; I am lucky to have found it and been able to write about it.

True Blue Aussie

There is a land down under, this I know for sure—'cause this is where I lived, not so long ago.

To be a "Dinky Aussie," you've just gotta put on your hats of blue; caps and scarves will mostly do, or even just our Akubra's.

"Gently does it," our saying goes. If your skin is pale and not yet tanned, one has to place upon their noses a screen so white—now, that is cool.

Covered in nets and swags on backs, hears our tunes of songs sounding out, sitting round campfires, crackling pots brews whispering mists sending water vapors up into the nights sky, the old billabong, awaits silently by.

"Sing 'em," said the cattlemen, "sing 'em, let them cattle quieten in the dewy night's air." "Them ole gum trees," whispers one, "wears the brunt of some wild 'n wooly winds in mountains far and wide."

Quench your thirst, your heart is here; our desert is a blooming. Waddle on down this barren inland, a water hole surprises most. Where grass is green and crocodiles live, young joeys on the hop, bouncing through mountains high on either side, cannons lead to waterfalls a gush, filling the land in summertime blues.

Stars slip silently by, glistering up high, listening to our heartbeat— notes played on didgeridoos. Sounds drift out, weathered in time… slowly drifting along now in silence!

Carol Swenson
Eustace, TX United States

Dreamer

I love how the sun shines so bright
There is beauty when the stars shine at night
Look at the moon, it glows like a light
The waves of the ocean roar and roll
The sun and the moon glisten on the midnight seas
Why is everyone staring at me?
I am enjoying God's beautiful weather, it is such a pleasure
I wish I could fly—fly high in the sky
I want to escape the cruelness of the cold, cold world
Wow, look at those mountains; they have holes
Are those human's walking below?
If so, they have no souls
Open your eyes, is this a dream?
Dreams are dreams, don't be afraid to let go
Get up, wake up from that dream
You are such a beautiful soul
Dreams are dreams, and dreaming
About the pleasant things will make you grow.

Sheila Crews
Memphis, TN United States

Say "No" to Domestic Violence

Before the domestic violence reaches its peak
it is help that I suggest you seek.
So, my love, I write this to you—
the abuse you inflict will no longer do.
You asked me to be in your life,
the violence cuts my heart like a knife.
Your heart seems full of rage,
time to put your anger in a cage.
The way you treat me is not right,
seems like all we do is fight.
You lash out without an excuse;
there is no reason for the abuse.
No longer will I take the violence
you expect me to take in silence.
Because your violence is driving me insane,
I put an end to all of this pain.
Your attitude, I can no longer ignore—
time for me to walk out the door!

Troy Allen Houston
Cheyenne, WY United States

Elements of Skitzophrantic Poetry

Influenced by generous transparencies, "nice" reviews, inoffensive,
ninety-seven percent ***** ratings for ostentatious absurdities on
poetry websites.

So it has come to this, my love
obtuse ravings, wanton sound, Picassan rantings, a form of
oxymoronic babblings abound

Unexpected anticipations, disillusioned imaginations
regimental emotions, accidental intentions, thoughtless cogitations
indirectly rhyming compositions

Free verse approaches
a two-year-old's finger-paint, while blank verse reproaches
an engineer's blueprint.

January—December
he say, she say; something they remember
we say, cliché

Potatoe, potato,
mama mia, tomatoe, tomato,
onomatopoeia

Whining cat calls, meow meow
random rhymes lacking rhythm, scattered meanings confound
disenchanting images, smitten with 'em

Elements unintended receiving praises
disfigured figures of speech, careless words and verbose phrases
undeserving flattery each

If Christopher Columbus could
discover the new world of poetry in the twenty-first century, he would
turn his ships around most hurriedly.

Robert McCluskey
Tampa, FL United States

Your Loss

Yeah, you missed out
You missed out on all of the memories
Swimming without floaties
Decorating our Christmas tree
My first day of school
My first loose tooth
Every amazing dream
Every frightening nightmare
My dreams and aspirations
My fears and uncertainties
All the yelling, screaming fights
All the loving, caring make-ups
My very first boyfriend
My once-in-a-lifetime first kiss
The first of many heartbreaks
The many, many tears
Thanks for leaving
Thanks for being the parent you promised you'd never be,
"Dad."

Sabrina Villanueva-Avalos
San Carlos, CA United States

Not Afraid

In this life You have choices
Some good and some bad
but the game isn't over just
because of the bad choices you made
You can stand up and raise above
the demons that are holding you down.
showing everyone you have the power to
face whatever the world tries to throw at you
Laughing at the world when all they have is
the past to throw at you
Knowing your stronger and can stand on your own
understanding
It's time to let all the skeletons out of your closet
Showing everyone your not afraid of the past mistakes
and you have nothing left to hide and you were down but
never out of the game .

Angela Heady
Curtisbay, MD United States

My Big Brother

You are always here for me.
Our memories of one another
Are good for me to keep
Do you remember when we were kids,
And I told you that I loved you? I still do.
I know at times we are not close, I know I strayed as far
But you were waiting for me there, every time I came to care.

My big brother, you see what I cannot.
You never would admit to it, but love is all we got
In a time of saddened sorrow, in a time of joy
You told me to look at tomorrow, you told me to employ
Love, and I have

My big brother, I love the way you speak
The way you laugh and play at life, the way you are not weak
The excitement that you bring to everything you do.
The air may faintly ring, the swallows, they may coo
To the sky; I can hear it when I fly.

My big brother, you'll never leave me here—
You stay with me forever, though now you disappear

My big brother, your skin is white as ash
Your touch is cold and brings a chill, no longer do you thrash
Bound up tight in ropes of white, laid to rest in wood
Sit there in the dark of night, against a wall I stood

My big brother, catch me when I fall
Lift me up when I am hurt, and come whene'er I call
We used to laugh and run around, now those days are through
Today, both of us are bound; there's not more I can do

My big brother, thank you for our time
You've heard my words and listened well, but here does end our climb
It was good to know you, they were my fondest years
If only I could show you you've triumphed all my fears
But one—the fear you would be gone

Nina Downey
Santa Barbara, CA United States

Love

I hate to see people in so much pain
There are things people do that cannot be explained
It breaks my heart to know what people can do
I wish there was something more I could do for you
If I had a magic wand I would make it go away
But unfortunately it does not work that way

Love hurts and people can be unfair
There is nothing else that can compare
But there is something you can do
Move on and not let it bother you
Easier said than done I know
But sometimes we just need to let things go

Don't blame yourself for anything at all
Don't let them take you down or make you fall
Don't look back or dwell in the past
You need to keep moving forward so you won't be last
You are stronger than you think you are
You have your life set and you will go far
Just keep holding on because it's not the end
You have your family and your friends

Ashley Barlow
Richmond, VA United States

I went through a really tough time in my life and writing poetry has been a great outlet for me. I am currently a college student and reside in Virginia. I play rugby for my school. I plan to continue writing and hope to make a difference in someone's life.

Succumb

As trees shed their shiftlessness
Shuddering sky shadowing ghosts
Grumbler shape illusions specters
Haphazardly convulsive robbery expectancy
Vibrant impulse humorously superstitiously
Nonchalant form and yet lusterlessness
Burdenless measure placements
Flowing nature slithering submissiveness
Excitement intrusion imperfectly spoken
Genealogy disguise impressing vaporization
Suddenly energetic cunningly inhalation
Extinguish breathing sedateness there leaves
Utter the mirror of the soul affirm silent
As ancestry arrogantly timidity succumb

Richard Cagg
Saint Joseph, MO United States

Richard retired as a postal worker. His hobbies are poetry, music, swimming, and tools. He plays guitar, bass and mandolin. He is quite involved in church, various organizations and was a counselor. He has been awarded forty-five prestigious major poetry awards—both national and international—and has been in Who's Who in Poetry three times on both the East and West Coast. Richard received an Honorary Congressional Award from the state of Missouri, and is Poet Laureate of Cameron, MI. He is a professional poet and author of eight books. He jokingly says he is a triple "P": preacher, poet, and postal worker.

Family Trouble

The world is full of unexpected things
It's crazy what each day brings
When life throws you a curve ball
Sometimes it's hard to give it your all
The events that come to pass day to day
The pain is the only thing that will stay
Relationships that we endure make it hard to cope
But we just have to hold on to some hope
That in time happiness will be in sight
And we will be ale to make things right
When nature is in charge sometimes it's wrong
It's our choice not to sing the same sad song
When the cards are dealt they do not lie
But to certain things we can say bye-bye
As long as we have love in our hearts
Sorrow will end and our life will start

Megan Labarthe
Westlake Village, CA United States

Poetry has always been my release. I am an ex-addict, and I'm trying to put my life back together. The emotions I feel are always very strong, and I'm most comfortable expressing them in the form of poetry. I've been writing for eleven years now, and I feel that my self-expression may help others in the sense that they can relate to what I'm saying, or it can help them through a hard time or give them hope.

Nature's Art

The willow breaks from the weight
Of the storm that came
And left its mark on nature's art
Though some was left the same.

The roses slipped away
From winter's frosty cold
The elm, its leaves upon the ground
At the touch of fall's first chill.

The heat of summer fervor
Will wilt the wild flower
And the new wheat will die
In springs often-wet attire.

It has its way in all we see,
Hear, touch, feel, or smell
Nature's brush, nature's art
No finer art than these.

James Scarr
Kent, WA United States

Dear Satan

Once there was a time I walked under your feet
Oh, vile one full of hate and deceit
You lied to me time and time again
You tried to convince me you were my only friend
All the while, you were plotting to kill me in the end
I must admit, you almost had me beat
Then Jesus came and stood before my feet
You are not alone, Jesus said. I am here for you my Father's child
I looked at Him and then I laughed
With the life I've led, surely You are mistaken
Then He touched me on the hand
The emptiness I felt tuned to Joy
I had been saved that very day
A child of God, proud to serve forever, I will be

Steve Ludwig
Holly Hill, FL United States

This was written at a time when I had just given my life back to Christ. I owe everything to God; He saved me from myself and from Satan's grasp. I wrote this so I would never forget.

A House by the Sea

He built me a house by the sea—
A tall, narrow house.
A sewing room for me,
a work room for him.
A smooth, mahogany piano
and a mantel clock that chimed the hour.
He built me a house by the sea—
A large house, high on a bluff.
Tearful windows locked
against frantic, high-flying waters.
Sleep came quickly in their roars and whispers.
He hammered a walkway above the roof-line;
I never knew it was called a widow's walk.
He built me a house by the sea.
One morning he left, smiling.
At least I had that.
I walked in circles
along my heaven's rail
in his scarf and gloves and heavy cape,
searching the endless ocean with a pounding heart—
The smell of him, my only comfort.
He built me a house by the sea.
I thank the angels for the time I had with him,
In the house that he built…by the sea.

Claire Cameron
Santa Cruz, CA United States

I began writing poetry at the age of eight, the same year in which I was fascinated by the theatre. Since that time, I have written multiple poems, published many, and been involved with several theatre companies—both as actor and stage director. Writing creates a place where I can go at any time, in any place, whether I'm sad or gloriously happy. Currently, I am artistic director for the Liliana Moraru Santa Cruz Jewish Theatre in Santa Cruz, CA—the first theatre of its kind on the central California coast. Being a writer of poetry has brought a tremendous sense of passion and a deeper understanding to my work as a theatre director. Ideas flow freely. I will always be grateful these abilities came into my life.

Ethereal to Physical

A stranger locked within a backlit space
Charming words, handsome, smiling face
Patient persistence until walls fell
Esoteric discoveries, by ask and tell
Awestruck by attraction
Never before felt by a fraction
Efflorescence of unknown zeal for another
Preternatural lure to each other
Devising life changes
Anticipation on abundant ranges
Luminescent grains of hope trickling through a vicious hourglass
Longing throughout each day for the next to pass
Disbelief of fruition
Promises kept during a seemingly endless mission
The immensely desired instant that became historic
An epic moment, unbelievably euphoric
Celestial bodies brought together
Once again, now and forever
More wondrous layers to learn
No more need to yearn
Beginning a highly coveted joined life
Soft, warm, living together—no longer cold and sharp as a knife
Each day filled with light
Every dusk becoming a comforting, contented night
Through the ether, adjacent to above
Two of a kind, reunited in love

Angelique Novak
Andover, MN United States

My spinal cord was injured in 1994 when I was thirteen, leaving me quadriplegic and ventilator-dependent. Afterwards, I thought I'd never have a loving, meaningful relationship with a man. That was until Brian found me and waited for me to believe I was worth being with and loved by someone who didn't have to. He, despite all I lack, moved his entire life for us to be together. I truly believe we've been together before, that the universe made sure we were reunited, and that we'll be together again. Even the most mundane things done together are dreams come true!

Isolation Row

The line is never-ending.
As we stand
One by one
In a line that will never move,
A line that will never speak.
The tales of sorrow,
Of pain,
Of abuse and neglect—
The songs of the innocent
That were wrongly accused
Are now forced to sing in their hearts.
For if they speak or make any noise
They will find you,
And they will part your sanity,
As well as decimate part of your soul.
There is no escape,
For once you enter the line,
The only way you can leave is a trade with your life.
It would be considered a miracle to escape with your soul,
Which would be concluded soon
By the warden's success in recapturing you—
Which leads to more silence,
More songs that are hidden
And eventually, words that are forgotten.

Gabrielle Lewis
Oxford, NY United States

Love and Joy

Love and joy, oh, love and joy
Love is faith, love is trust
Love never questions or argues
Love never gets angry or harsh or mean
Love is never jealous or envious
Love is never anxious or worried
Love is always merciful and forgiving
Love is compassionate, cheerful and praising
Love is sincere, love is joy
Love is God
Joy is a child's prayer or laughter
Joy is a wonderful surprise
Joy is a friend with a smile, on a miserable day
Joy is water in the desert
Joy is arms of forgiveness
Love and joy go hand in hand
Love and joy are never-ending
As they lead us up home
To God and Heaven and eternal life
From everlasting to everlasting

Eric Barkley
Highland Park, NJ United States

This is my first ever poem. It was written on my grandfather's birthday, Jan. 26, 1973. I was ten years old, and I have been writing ever since. I am now fifty years old and have over 800 poems to my credit. I also write short stories and have written almost twenty plays. I dedicate everything I write to God as a thank you for His great gift.

Who Am I?

Do you know who am I?
Everyone needs me daily,
I am supposed to be everybody's friend.

You need me daily to be healthy;
make me your friend if you can,
even if sometimes you may think
I am hard to come by.

My name is Laughter, everyone knows me.
Anyone who embraces me knows how sweet I am;
I make everyone feel good.
Make me part of your life—
you will be glad you did.

Veronica Masilo-Makotoko
Toronto, ON Canada

I have always thought poetry is for certain kinds of people; I never thought I would find myself writing poems. In high school, I did not have any idea how poets composed their work. With this opportunity, I am learning to find my inner creativity. My poem is about laughter; I decided to write about it, because I realize it's what keeps me going in my daily life. I hope the readers enjoy my poem.

An Ode to a Sparkle and a Teardrop

The impossible couplet in impossible times
That we were, an inordinate mi
An Aries woman and a Pisces man
Intertwined in an odd, ethereal fix
Supernatural with mind-reading power
I would start to say…and she completing
Even time itself stood still for us
That first day we met, a full moon retreating
Bonnie brought light and brilliance to the set
I gave strength and somewhat the norm
So alike, yet so different were we
A poetic couplet in human form
My Bonnie lass this life did pass
Her world is now another
Now I pray from day to day
And put one foot in front of the other
I start to say, it comes to naught
The completion of thoughts has gone
I sit and think of words to write
The ink in my pen turns to stone
Now late at night I look to the stars
To find that twinkle in her eye
My muse, I find, a teardrop falls
She's at the side of Lady Di!

Douglas Varner
Cleveland, TN United States

My wife Bonnie was an inspiration to many. She got me started writing again. Sadly, she passed away March 3, 2006 before learning I was first published as a poet; she was my soul mate. In 2009, I almost died from carbon monoxide poisoning. I was in the emergency room for hours being fed one hundred percent oxygen to bring me out of it. During that time, Bonnie sat at the foot of my bed, looking over me. I started coming around, and she came over and touched my cheek and kissed me on the forehead before she left. She is still looking over me.

Changing into a New Season

The air chilled with the first signs of fall
Dripping into the reminiscence of summer

The wind painted the leaves overnight
Transforming the world into its canvas

As the nights chilled, the days grew shorter
Allowing the newly reborn season to leave its mark

Frost has struck once again, freezing the tears of the clouds
Showing no one mercy

The world changed heavy as snow
Though children played with Old Man Frost, and dreamt
Of Old Saint Nick, they longed for the warm kiss of the sun again

Samantha Glisson
Spokane, WA United States

Leaving

Please, just walk away
I don't want you anymore
It's better off this way

I know it'll be okay
I'm sorry I'm a whore
Baby, please just walk away

I can't do this one more day
You've become such a bore
Trust me, it's better off this way

I met you back in May
But now it's time to close the door
So, please, just walk away

I've run out of words to say
Crushed you right down to your core
And it's better off this way

I've found a new place to lay
Down the hill, by the moor
So, please, just walk away
It's better off this way

Marina Daily
Caldwell, ID United States

You Will Regret

You will regret...
That you made me cry
That you didn't see your love in my eye
That you failed my heart and didn't even try
You will regret and soon you will know why
You will regret and miss my smiles
When I will be away from you a hundred or a thousand miles
You think I am not your candidate now and not your style
You will miss my soul, my laughter it won't be a while
You will regret...believe me...I don't want you to
Regrets are something that I don't wish for you
You said that I am your soul mate
Explained our love was our great fate.....
A day later, I was left on the side...all your love and care did subside
Sorry I didn't know how to play your game
My innocence and good heart you can only blame..
You will regret that you had me one day
You will see my picture and wonder how you didn't stay
You will regret that you couldn't touch me anymore
You will regret that you never truly opened your heart door
You will regret me forever...you will never see me again, never
You will Regret me today and tomorrow
Hope you can live well with your sorrow
Goodbye now I have to go my way
Goodbye now is all what I have to say

Shahinaz Soliman
Palos Verdes Estates, CA United States

I am a physician who loves art and poetry. I was born and raised in Cairo, Egypt and started writing poetry at the age of eight in both English and Arabic. I started medical school at the age of sixteen and continued to write poetry throughout all my school years. I moved to the United States when I was twenty-four years old and continued my medical career. My love for art, music and poetry has always been my passion; I try to apply my artistic side in my medical practice in Southern California. My life hardships and happiness have inspired me, as well as the political situation in Egypt and the suffering of the Coptic Christians there; I was encouraged and inspired to write many poems to express our feelings.

One of a Kind

Summer disappears
Autumn leaves
Winter passes
Spring arrives
She remains strong

Her beauty never fades
Her devotion to the sun never seizes
Her love for the bees never dries

Sunshine heats
Storms roar
Snow falls
Rain drizzles
She continues to worship her Creator

Her pedals are colorful
Her leaves are open wide
Her steam is unbreakable

She is among weeds
But not alone
She is unique
But not estranged
She is truly one of a kind

Kamila Narrainen
Montreal, QC Canada

I'm twenty-nine years old, and I aspire to be writer. I am passionate about writing and reading. On June 12, 2004, I was admiring nature, and the thought of writing a poem about a flower came to my mind. Something as small but yet beautiful as a flower can say so much.

The Beauty of Autumn

The days are getting shorter
Autumn is here
The days are getting colder
Jack Frost is everywhere

The leaves are turning red, gold and brown
As the strong howling wind, blows
Them twirling to the ground

Walnuts are falling from the trees
Everywhere
As the autumn breeze fills the air

The buck and the doe run through
the woods side by side
As they hold their heads up, full
of pride

The squirrels play tag in the beautiful
fallen leaves
As they run and play in the autumn
breeze

The beauty of autumn just takes
my breath away
On such a beautiful, autumn day

Bobbi Jo Hager
Ozark, AL United States

Pockets

A little boy, head hung down
When asked, "Why?"
He turned around:
No pockets in my pants, Ma

For pretty sticks and leaves
an odd-colored stone
for my cars and crayons
that keep me company
when I'm all alone

Pockets are great things, you know
to warm your hands when they are cold
for old pop bottle caps
and candy wrapped in foiled gold

Here's pockets in your pants, son
with a happy grin and a sweet thank you
the innocence of a babe
His feet a dancing, hazel eyes laughing
what a difference pockets made!

Marcy Bowser
Newark, OH United States

I love writing poetry; it is like making music with words. I wrote this poem several years ago—it was archived on a poetry website but never published. This poem is one of my favorites, as I wrote it about my son when he was little.

My Life

My bones are still attached, although I am dead.
They put poison in my drink...I believe they called it lead?
They did not see me then, and they do not see me now;
It was as if I was a ghost in the crowd.
Although they knew I died,
They still did not cry—
For I am the only one who visits my grave,
Where they buried me in a cave.
They destroyed my life and didn't care,
Now I wonder elsewhere.
For I am lonely and I am lost;
I must find true love with myself all covered in moss.
Some say that it's among the living but I did not find it then...
Now I must look for it among the dead.
Although I am invisible, some see that I exist,
But only if you look in the cold, dark mist.
Those of you who are superstitious, you may see me weep;
But those who are not may think I am a creep.
My life is at end, but there is something you must know:
You must follow your heart even in the dark, if it must be so.
I love the world, but it seems as if they hate me.
Now I must go and flee.

Teresa Millard
Branford, FL United States

I love to write poems—they are one of the ways I express myself. Most of my poems are about love. I don't just sit around trying to think of what to write about, it just comes to mind at random moments. That's when I grab a pen and write down what's on my mind, before I forget it.

Those Moments...

Those moments
Where after trying so hard
For so long
To hold it all in
You just can't anymore
Those moments
When after giving so much
Throwing your heart at it
Thrusting your soul upon it
You realize it was all wasted
Those moments
When the walls you've built
So high
So strong
Just come crashing down
Those moment
Where you have nothing
Save your mistakes
And your fears
And nowhere left to turn
Those moments
Where all you can do,
Is let go
Break down
And cry

Logyn Smith
Selinsgrove, PA United States

Erasing Borders

A man of true character
And a child with strong spirit
Came face to face at a country border—
Though missing on the ground of commonality
Were culture, language and nationality.

Owing to precious moments spent
Educating and caring for community,
Encouraging each others' heart and mind,
The common space opened the border gate
Permitting liberation of predestined fate.

Through selfless acts of open love,
Their hearts grew and blossomed free;
Hence, when he had nurtured a child in need,
A smile of gratitude planted a seed
In the man who at last understood his deeds.

Lines that separate
And borders which divide
Can only be erased if love is pure—
Allowing many to join hands together
In the quest to wipe out poverty, forever.

Theresa Kannenberg
Gifu City, Gifu Prefecture Japan

Theresa and her family live in Gifu, Japan, where she is teaching English as a foreign language at various universities. She is also the owner of TLC English Center as well as a Hado instructor/Hado counselor and spiritual wellness practitioner. She has co-created a poetry book with her sister's photography, called A Symphony of Words and Images, Two Sisters, Worlds Apart, Creative Together, which is available on Amazon.com. Theresa hopes her work will inspire you to pursue life with renewed vision and to experience love and gratitude in each and every day of your lives. You are blessed and have the power to touch others with your love.

Limbo

Lost, swimming in a sea of night
darkness of the depths engulfs me—

Forcing me to fall deeper and deeper into
the dark, black abyss awaiting me.

Scream, but that only entraps my lungs
with water. Unable to move for air, I become paralyzed.

The darker the water I enter, the murkier it becomes.
I can't find my way through the black depths; I am
surrounded in a haze of blue and black.

I am all alone. No one can help me to the surface—
No rope, no line to bring me home.

Thrust, punch, kick as I may, I am thwarted,
unable to do any damage.

So slowly, I succumb to the abyss—embracing the
cold and unbearable that you have pushed me into.

I succumb to the sea by the hand of my love.

Sarah Cohen
Spiro, OK United States

Together

We have the past, you and I—
Bright red,
Shedding its warming light into the darkened corners
Of whatever cold may come.

We hold a prize,
Far greater than winning all;
A trophy, to polish, to hold, to cherish
Over our forever fireplace

We share a dream
To eclipse all other dreams,
To escape reality forever—
Moments, preserved in the rich clear amber
Of what we are.

We covet a knowledge
Unique in its sphere
Of mutual understanding.

Let us move forward, extend;
Enrich the world, all those we touch,
With the treasures we have found
By giving only everything
All,
To each other.

Gordon Vaughan
New York, NY United States

The Senior Citizens

Alive with seniority, full of glory
After hitting seventy can be a party!
Reservations are required…no special favors
Whatever you've acquired belongs to lawyers!

The nursing homes pre-sell some bodies
They're on loan for research facilities!
No one listed for any emergencies?
Don't get pissed…Pampers are luxuries!

Seniors are harassed and treated badly
Maybe their past was really ugly?
Mouth is toothless…waiting to die
They feel useless, tired and dry!

Each day comes, dragging their feet
Then day is gone…back to sleep!
Some live on, with peaceful heart
Others have gone for being smart!

Physicians do tests, protecting their liability
They care less about your disability!
Some have degrees, years of experience
They can squeeze…your parent's inheritance!

Bad cholesterol high, So are medications
Then it's goodbye…dead from complications!
Some seniors complain, they grow bitter
Their permanent domain? The Devil's shelter!

Maria Chevalier
Cape Coral, FL United States

Monster

In my dreams I am the monster
The tyrant, preying on sweat and flesh
Teeth gnawing desperately at hope
A black shadow of fear sauntering over
Every soul
Every home
Gently gnashing on skin and bone
I stagger toward the moonlight
And howl out all my fears
No sounds of birds or pretty skies
Just death, lust, fire and painful lies
I run from me
That evil beast, who trudges on
Determined to take innocence away
I'm not holy, but I pray
For anyone to hear my plea
"Please, just please save me from me!"
I'm not the devil
Or a lurid shadow
A demon who would deem
All happiness and innocence
The monster in my dreams

Sabrina Espaillat
Paterson, NJ United States

The Sound of Silence

Walking along the beach is lovely,
while walking holding hands with a partner
with the sound of silence,
I enjoy watching the waves,
and listening to the splash of water that goes to and fro.
Verily, the scene is soothing;
It gives pleasure and delight.
In the midst of a summer day,
the sun is at its peak.
It illuminates the earth we live in,
that allows people to accomplish goals.
What a glorious day!
Along the way, there are logs on the ocean shore,
trees that add beauty to surroundings,
and flock of birds that glide in the atmosphere
with the sound of silence.
I can't stop admiring the creation of God—
His creativity that is amazing
and wonderful gives life to living things.

Rosario Roberts
Olympia, WA United States

Ghost of Christmas

The record spins, my ears get tight
my heart goes heavy as our song starts
Memories of your wrinkled hands holding mine flood my head
I can almost feel your feet beneath mine
I hum, just as you did, and smile as I turn
The ghost of your arm is pressed against my back

But this time I have tiny toes on top of mine
Leading our turns as we dance to the tune
"I'm dreaming of a white Christmas, just like the ones I use to know"
Every Christmas will be our Christmas, as it was before
Even with you gone, our dance will always live on

Marisa Davila-Walston
San Diego, CA United States

You take different experiences from life and use them to help mold into the person you are; I am taking these experiences from my life and molding them into pieces of art. I hope you take things from my work to help in the molding of your life.

Question in Ignorance

Buried deep into earth by the ageless time
I have lived so long, enough to build mountains on me
with a thirsting quest to reach out and soar
over the years, I have waited for the chance to explode...
like a seed that grows, tearing the ground to transform into a tree
I needed to see what I could be
waxing and waning with the energies of search
I began to climb up, meditating within
asking the Lord again and again, what have You made me to be?
In silence did He respond. Burning me more with vigor and thirst
On a day, I burst with energies red and hot!
I would reach the sky, I thought
only to fountain and become a black rock!
Sun, moon and the stars are having a laugh at me, was my only thought
Gloomed in dejection, I cried in despair
Oh! Merciful, this is what You want me to be?
Countless pleas did I make; silence is what he talked
Over time in acceptance and thought, embraced that I was a black rock!
Silence now is what I kept with, my Lord
I began to settle as the black rock
Detached over appearance, I retraced the road of search within
in heat and cold did my body wash...sternly I continued my walk
A gush of happiness and content did I suddenly experience
I opened my eyes to see and found my twinkle...
In innocence I did ask (the God): who I could be?
First time ever did He say, "You are my diamond"

Roshini Velamuri
Williamsville, NY United States

Professionally I am a data architect/software engineer. Over the years, the experiences I've had, things I saw and people have always inspired the "larger than life" idea. Sometimes, I see a lot of people around me, including myself, asking/ seeking the purpose of existence: who am I made to be? When we reflect back, we find the purpose. Such thoughts inspired me to write "Question in Ignorance." In addition to poetry I also enjoy painting and dancing. You can find more of my work on my website: http://roshini-studio-d.com/

A Red Bird in the Snowing Day

The ground was covered with foot-high snow
The light flakes still fell scarcely
Looking at a leafless tree far in the back yard
I was surprised to see a red leaf
Hung on a top-bald branch
Waving in the breezy air
Wriggling among snow threads
It was the only leaf left in the leafless woods
It must be the last leaf of the year
The uniqueness dominated the decayed world

Yet, it did not sway on the rhythm of wind
It did not flip in the direction of snowfall
It kept still at one gust blow
It swirled in the motionless of branches

A naughty chirping woke me up from my foliage dream
It was a red bird
A tiny, crimson creature
In the snowing day
Flapped to adjust its position
Twisted to arrange its feather
Stretched to look at the pure, white landscape
Its deep curiosity enlightened the lonely winter
Its flaming energy warmed the snowing day

It is a pre-spring wish for the prospecting year.

Wen-Yang Tsay
Bridgewater, NJ United States

Wen-Yang Tsay is a civil engineer who currently works for MTA. His hobbies are literature and art. He likes to write poems about natural scenery.

Nowhere to Run

When life takes a turn for the worst
and you just want to hide or run,
you feel there is nowhere else to go,
so why not cry out to God's Son?
You feel so lost and alone,
not sure of the road you should take.
Uncertain of how you arrived here...
did you make some kind of mistake?
Don't focus on all that is wrong;
try to find what is right.
And go back to the place it all started,
when day turned to darkest night.
Cry out to Jesus with your heart,
tell Him just how you feel;
don't hold anything back,
it's all part of helping you heal.
He sees the tears you have cried
and knows you so very well.
So take it all to Lord Jesus—
every problem and fear you can tell.
As you allow him to heal you,
new experiences he will show.
So run into the arms of Jesus,
His love for you will continue to flow.

Michelle Simmons
Port Pirie, SA Australia

Amor Florum et Fiat Mundi

Amor florum et fiat mundi
Witness man's contempt in heated fight
Through pillars of strength, compassion, and endless light
The life of one seems small in comparison
When grass covers the skin
And time wrinkles the bones
What will the living say?
Will they dance the dances
and sing the songs?
Will they understand
History is ours
But it is not truth
Not in the eyes of the world
Those eyes see much more
Every moment in time is calculated by the slowly winding daisy
and the ever-spinning oak tree
To care about nothing
seems like such bliss
Reanimations of death
and the regeneration of life
Constant
To be a man
To look at the road ahead
and have the same thoughts that roses ponder
Ponder the minerals of Mother Earth
I hope to find you, Mother
I hope to dig the earth
Your earth
Do not take much time to think about only others
You must think for yourself
But you must think about yourself only in the company of strangers
Then you will see, the importance of others
Rush of waves
And pink hills
And pearl stars
Amor florum et fiat mundi

Sean Perlman
Bethlehem, PA United States

Lost Soul

I am lost
wandering through the crowd
hoping to be noticed
but I'm starting to drown

If I do wrong
everyone will see
If I do right
no one will believe
that it was me

That I am capable
of adding to the equation
I only get subtraction
until I'm left in the red
lacking any benefits
except in someone's bed

Is that all I am
nothing more?
I am left feeling
like your whore
only here for your need
expecting something in return
feeling full of greed
knowing only the burn of your indifference

Amanda Julian
Circleville, OH United States

A Face in the Mob

Saw a face in the mob, fists clenched, raising upwards
Unkempt hair flaring like the flames, agitated like hurricane
At the fizzy crest of the mob, I saw, a phosphorescent glow
on that familiar face in the mob
When the rout dispersed in a whorl, amidst the lowered
hands and the hasty footmarks, of the mob, she was lost somewhere
That familiar face in the mob
It comforts me, remembering, the long, glossy black hair
mostly straight, with a few curls and waves at the end
Eyes to match, the blackest of all blacks. High cheekbones
set directly under her eyes, bottom lashes brushing against
them every time she blinks. A roundish nose and a defined
jawline ending in a small chin. Tiny, delicate lips completed by
a beauty mark above and to the left
But their hands are fallen, and at the fizzy apex of the mob
I can't see the phosphorescent glow. Not anymore
When faces, are trying to hide the distortion, under the thick covers
of luxurious maquillage, when they are using the elite scents to hide
the disgusting stench of the decomposing, dead bodies
There, her peaceful face, a sign of harmony, wakes me up from my
    slumber
And I, in the darkness, hand everyone the circumscribed flyers
to demolish the very foundation of this decrepit building
So that familiar face can find a body in the mob
and the unshackled love of all the beings can find a way
through the bridge between two hearts

Robin Asati
Pune, Maharashtra India

I was born into an Indian family on December 3, 1983, and grew up in Balaghat, a sleepy town in Central India. I am the son of Ashok and Sandhya Asati. I have one younger brother, Happy. I am a business graduate and currently working as a research analyst with a financial MNC. I am married, and my wife Tanvi is my biggest motivation and inspiration for writing. I have three self-published collections of poetry: Resuram (2007), And Hence I Grew (2009), and Memories of Another Day (2005). Apart from writing, I like music and play keyboard for my band.

The Immigrant Equilibrium

When I was sixteen
for a valid reason
I left my land
and migrated.
Sixteen years I lived in Emilia
and thirty in Toscana.
I do not feel Toscana
nor do I feel Emiliana.
Retired I will be some day
a house I will have
where well I will live.
I will build it on the ridge
where there is the conjunction
from the land of adoption
to the land of birth.
If I look out my window
I see my Toscana
if I look on the other side
I see my birth land.
I do not feel Toscana
nor do I feel Emiliana
but my equilibrium
I want to find in Frignano
Land I loved so much!

Diana Tosetti
Stuart, FL Italy

Only Heaven Would Know

only Heaven knows
who comes and goes
and what must be
to help us through this thing called life
and find eternity

tho here and now
you'll find some how
the things you must do
to take your place, within his grace
when Heaven welcomes you

if you open your heart
you will find
 when god receives you
he leaves your sins behind

then you'll walk in the sunlight
where the roses grow
and share the love
only Heaven would know

Donald Richards
Heath, OH United States

Moments

Lingering moments shared with another,
Moments untrampled by life's hectic pace.
Moments, immortal in memory's keeping
Are indelible imprints on yesterday's face.
For today is the reincarnation of the past,
And yesterday's gladness continues to dwell
In lingering moments shared with another,
In tomorrow's awakening to yesterday's thrill.
So precious the moments we share with each other!
Tomorrow seems almost a lifetime away—
For yesterday's shadow embraces the dawning
Of lingering moments we'll live for today.

Barbara Buehler
Lindenwold, NJ United States

The Life of Pain

The sound of rain
Brings back the pain
Of all the memories we shared
Even though my heart still beats
I know you never cared
I look at your picture with open eyes
Knowing everything was lies
As tear run down my face
I noticed the quietness of this place
The laughter has stopped ringing
The love has stopped singing
I must leave here in haste

Codi Witt
London, KY United States

Your Everything

I would like to be the wind
that propels you to your greatest height
gently embrace your wings
as you begin to take flight
The shoulder you cry on
when going through life trials
The reason you go on
and continue to smile.
The water that baptized
and cleansed you from within
The one you call
when you need your best friend
The dream that finds you
and keeps you awake
The reason for being
every breath you take
No, this is no delusion
I'd just like to think
You've come to the conclusion
I'm your everything

Darrell R. Heath Sr.
Saluda, SC United States

The Love of My Life

I met the love of my life seven years ago;
Why I let him go, I will never know.
He is the only man who has ever completed me—
When I'm with him I am happy and feel so free.
I have been in love with him for all these years,
I've had good memories, but they always produce tears.
No words can describe how great he makes me feel...
I've regretted walking away and felt like a heel.
When he touches me, it sends chills up my spine;
All I want is a chance to see if he'll once again be mine.
He's the only man I will love for the rest of my life,
I've had an ache in my heart for so long, like a dull knife.
I was the luckiest woman on earth for being with him,
Without him, the light at the end of the tunnel is so dim.
He started out as and still is my best friend,
I will love him unconditionally, until the very end.
I honestly believe what brought us together was fate,
I hope and pray every day that it's not too late.
I don't know what he did to make me feel this way,
But I thank God for having him back in my life everyday.
There is something absolutely wonderful about you
Please don't ever change, always stay the perfect you.
I never want our happiness and love to stop,
You honestly are the love of my life, Scott!

Jennifer Hardesty
Battle Ground, IN United States

I got my ability to write poetry from my grandfather. All of my poems have to do with my family, feelings, and life experiences. My children and the love of my life have been a great inspiration to me.

One Love

I cannot wait for you to see
Just how much you mean to me
One dress, one tux, and two rings
Will bind this love together above all things

Down the aisle stands a man you believe in
At the other end is a woman I see no end
In the middle there are people who came to see
This man and this woman join in matrimony

At last I have found the one to love
Sent down from Heaven high above
To have and to hold and cherish
Symbolized by a ring of gold

Bryan Coil
Tempe, AZ United States

*I started writing poetry when I was in high school as a way to pass the time. Now
I write as a way to express and communicate when I cannot find the right words.*

Say Goodbye to Mediocrity

The answers to the universe lie within our souls.
I smelled the roses, and tasted them too.
I sensed a presence, that was stronger than me...
Do we choose to be a knight at the round table,

Or a peasant in the field?
The choices are ours to make.
We determine what we want
In life, and then stand for that.

We're in good company, if we choose well.
Think about the creatures that live in the trees:
There are many species, that each tree gives shade
and shelter to. Live life as well as the tree—

Say goodbye to mediocrity, and hello to what's true.
There is a fifth element (*love*) and a final spin to the story,
Which involves *you*. Our world as we know it is changing
And ever will be; but, it is up to us to make a difference, you see.

Keep praying, believing God is with us, He loves us,
He stands for *truth*. God is the Father, and Jesus Christ
Is His Son; The Holy Spirit was sent to guide us, each and everyone.
Envision God's light filling each heart with love...

I smelled the roses and remember that fragrance,
It lingers and lifts my spirit still.
(I dance with delight, and my mind is awakened to the
Possibilities that abound!) God is my God, and He is still around!

Peggy Beeber
Lago Vista, TX United States

I Scream

I scream as I come into this life, and this is my beginning
I scream with joy when I learn to ride my bike—training wheels are
    gone
I scream and throw my cap as I graduate from high school
I scream with glee when I meet the man of my dreams; I am blessed
I scream in pain when I bear my child, but it changes my life forever
I scream and giggle with my best girlfriend; our secrets are endearing
I scream with grief when I lose my mom—how can I bear the
    heartache?
I scream with sadness as I hear the prognosis. This cannot be true!
I scream, I scream, silently I scream as I ponder the life I lived
My final scream has mixed emotions—I've lived, I've loved, I've died

Pearlene Derello
Mebane, NC United States

I' Nd

To sum up the era with all I
have within my mind,
 I look all around, eyes open
and shut only to find
 We still have not realized the
greatest gift is to be kind.
 To your friends and your enemies,
you must be inclined
 To keep one eye turned within to
see your heart is not blind.
 Some, it is obvious, will be left
in the dark—left behind
 To chew the fat, to fight it out
to peel back the rind.
 To expose the truth: that it was
all of us who caused the bind.
Forgetting our divine light love
while we wined and dined
 On our mother, whose only worth
was believed to be mined—
 Who was only seen as a machine
for pockets to be lined
 For shame! For all here and within
which we pined
 In the end will be that for which
we pine.

Jeremy Josey
Mt. Pleasant, ON Canada

When the Dragon Comes

Beasts and beauties all alike will eat you whole and wear your might.
They'll laugh at your love's embrace and run for fun to watch you chase.
Then stop in silence, see you come, and trap you under beating drums.
The noise, vibrations—deafening enough to rock your brutal being.

It is to say that they won't care; they'd watch your body, bloody, bare.
They want the prize, that stipulation that justifies your degradation.
That fertile cause of so much fuss that makes the turmoil gone like dust.

You're going off to fight a war that comes on fronts not seen before.
These people: nice, strong, beautiful, intelligent, dumb as a rock,
But all ready for the annihilation of their souls
For in this game, no boundary is told.

So forget your heart while in the scene, whether or not you're in a team.
Remember to use your greatest talents, gifts, and all the like,
And fly this game just like a kite
On a string upon your finger; if someone betrays, don't let them linger.
Then seize the prize and rise like cream
That parallels your sparkling gleam.

Then when you're on the ropes of doubt, you let the dragon within
    come out.
And belt upon the unsuspecting the fiery blaze they were suppressing.
Under the menacing, blazing pressure comes fiery diamonds like a
    thresher
To cut your competition to size; at this point, there's no compromise.

You'll take your seat upon your throne, know that this will set your
    tone.
It'll be a war, you know that well—but you will see them all in hell.

Erick Angarita
La Habra, CA United States

Can I Call You?

Can I call you Darling?
Can I call you Dear?
I'm looking for a word
You might like to hear

Could it be Sweetheart?
Could I call you Babe?
I'll call you Beautiful
Because you really are

But you are Charming
Delightful and Dazzling too
As well as being Wonderful
So what's a bloke to do?

It's written in the stars
Way up above
We'll find it in the music
So I think I'll call you Love

Peter Hayburn
Dubbo, NSWAustralia

Untitled

Teddy bear so old so worn
comfort me till you can't no more
My old tears rest deep into your fur
holding my memories I wish never more
Outfit you wear lets me know
I will always have my family near
Your little arms rested over mine
as I held you tight trying to hide from
the monsters who stalked me in my dreams
You keep all my secrets, and you never judge me
You still rest in my grasp, every time I fall asleep
Please never leave me, my teddy bear; you are the one that's always
    there
Even now that I'm sixteen, you are still my safety line
Letting me know you still will listen, no matter what I say
I take you everywhere, I need you by my side
I hid you in my backpack my first day of kindergarten
you sat in my lap when I cried because my dog just died
You don't say a word when I need to vent
nor when I cry and beg to forget
I just hold you tight, and I know everything will be alright
My Mary bear, don't ever leave me
You are my one and only—my longest friend, softest pillow, and best
    hug
I love you so, even though a teen I am
I will never let you go, no matter what happens in my life
I love you so, my teddy bear

Mandy Winzenried
High Bridge, NJ United States

What Is It?

Backflip, triple jump, handstand,
I sound like a gymnast.
I'm definitely not that;
I don't have the eloquent finesse.

I'm dizzy and giddy,
Can't walk in a straight line.
I sound drunk—
But alcohol around me, you'll find no sign.

I am so happy,
I find everything funny.
Am I stoned?
For that, I don't have the money.

What is wrong with me?
I'm just not right.
Ah, I finally worked it out.
It's love that is in my sight.

Rowena Fox
Port Augusta, SA Australia

I am a country girl at heart who is full of goodwill, fun and love, for friends, family and the wonderful world in which we live. I have been inspired by my grandpa's love and appreciation of words, poetry, and verse. I have followed in his footsteps of turning words into meaningful prose. I have been writing poetry since I was about fourteen, and now at thirty, I find it a great emotional release and escape from the world in which we live.

Faces All Around Me

Faces all around me, talking about who I should be
What they do not realize is I am me
Hardships and battles I have fought
Lessons to learn that I need to be taught
People around me, too quick to judge
I will not even dare to budge
Yes, I'm short but who are you
to try and make me look like the fool?
Faces all around me, talking about who I should be
What they do not realize is: I am me
Bruises and broken bones I have faced
I still live on, day after day
I am a girl who is very smart
People do not realize I have a broken heart
Faces all around me, talking about who I should be
What they do not realize is I am me

Ashley Owen
Hendersonville, TN United States

The Fairy

"I saw a little fairy!" she whispered in my ear
As I bent down to kiss her and hold her, oh, so near.
Her eyes were so wide open, innocent and blue—
As if they begged me to believe what she had said was true.
I tucked her covers to her chin, caressed her forehead light,
Then whispered back, "I'm sure you did!" and kissed my own
goodnight.

Ruth Helton
Twin Falls, ID United States

These Questions I Ask

Can my heart physically break?
Why do tears instantly spring to my eyes?
Why can I only see the end
When I think of you?

How do I get past the pain?
Can I remember the happy times?
Is it possible to smile instead of cry
When I think of you?

Why do I feel lonely?
Am I the only one with this grief?
Will it ever subside
When I think of you?

How much time will this take
To look back and smile
To have my heart fill with love
When I think of you?

Courtney Wuthnow
Hesston, KS United States

Always and Forever

Perched on a windowsill,
The light from the heavens burst through the clouds
And streamed in outlining your beautiful silhouette.
You could hold my gaze forever
Because you're beautiful,
Because in your arms is an eternity of
Love,
Security,
Trust.
Always and forever
Your eyes will penetrate my soul,
My spirit,
My being.
They melt away the pain and the anger
As the sound of your voice
Fills the corners of my heart with ecstasy.
Your touch sends a shiver up my spine.
The soft embrace of your lips,
Me wanting to be consumed in them—
Consumed in you,
Always and forever.

Paige Noel
Brooklyn, NY United States

As a child, I always loved to write creatively and make stories come alive with my words. Every experience I had was documented as a poem, until I went to high school; my academics demanded more of time. Since then, I only write when inspiration comes.

Memories

So much we have gotten through
not for a blink do we see
A simple task that lies ahead
But indeed a rough one that passes smoothly
'Cause in the end, the turnout is fate
All based on our judgment and wishes
And wonder about what we want most
and have faith for the new day
Where memories are set aside
To make room for the new
And whilst we suffer the worst of pains
We grab our memories and strangle the dark
And hope for a deeper breath in the morning

John Bailey
Poquoson, VA United States

I am inspired to write poems by love and love lost and the positive outlook on all of it. No matter what, fate will turn out to give us what we want most. I hope my poems will inspire others to look forward in life. My life has been a rough route, and it could be worse. But in the long run, things turn out for the better, and the experience is worth it.

A Whisper of Candy

Her name is like a candy
It feels so sweet
As it rolls off my tongue
Like a cherry
With a hint of lemon drop
So smooth it seems
As if it could last forever
I savor every moment
I whisper the name
Kara Mae

Jonathan Cutcher
Santa Rosa, CA United States

This poem is dedicated to my girlfriend, Kara Romriell. We met each other in high school at Santa Rosa High, the city in which I was born and raised. It is she whom I would like to thank, firstly, for supporting my poetic ability every step of the way. I would also like to thank my mother for making this all possible. Without these two people brightening my world, day in and day out, I never would have had the honor of publishing my work internationally. I love you both with all my heart. And I hope you, the reader, enjoy this poem as much as I do.

Handwritten

You were the joy of my great-grandmother
Her tears hidden in the draping of the skirt—
While waiting for news from the front.

And the blush with which my mother pulled you out
of the chaos of a bouquet of roses on that morning of March.

And my younger sister's cry when you said: This is over.

And the tiny, crumpled grace that matched a number
with a smile in the crowd.

And that Robert Frost verse that we used to trick the hours;
and the popular songs that we all used to learn.

Oh, what a remote calmness moved us to tinker
the content on your striped form.

What an ancient wisdom you used to bring us a
longed lock, or the pale sepia color of an unseen face.

You, who privately and potently witnessed
the times of so many, dreamed inside the keepsake boxes of all....

It seems that you are dying, that you parted,

And we let you go like a forgotten ruin
Let go of a pair of staring brown-eyes.

With what sorrow we welcomed this uniformed character
that is envious of your soul.

Wendy Gomez
Boca Raton, FL United States

Welcome

Lakshmi Chamundeswari Devi Kundem
Sliding sparkling drops on the soft green silk,
Drank deep down, intoxicated Greenland
Stretching its welcome to the sky—limitless
Noised nest with twittering calls,
Leaping hearts with wings unfurled
Sending a musical band to the eastern sky.
Dark shades in groves, silent clusters,
Spectators, speechless at the opening
Marvel of the vast blue, everlasting
Miracle for a human heart,
Draped in dark, blue waters
Ready to unveil, to wash off,
To shine in thy golden hue
Each joyful heart, singing and dancing
Ever-shining richness, for the hearts wondering
How a moment's touch, leaves wealth
For a lifetime, immortal peace for a redemption
Celebration boundless for the moments endless

Devi Kundem
Vijayawada, Andhraprdesh India

I very much like nature poetry. I sought my inspiration from William Wordsworth's nature poetry. I am so inspired seeing nature. Sometimes, I feel I am born for nature. I am a lecturer, and I like to teach poetry. I forget my time when I teach poetry. I always feel there is a semblance between my childhood days and nature. Nature takes me back to my cherished memories and comforts me, soothes me and gives me back my preciousness in life. What more do I have to offer nature than this poetry?

I Remember When

I remember when
your words sounded oh, so sweet
you wined and dined me
as we danced in the streets
I was full of hopes and dreams
as you swept me off my feet.

Now I hear your name and shudder
tears come to my eyes
false promises, lies, broken dreams
lay dying in the street
abandonment for another
nothing was as it seemed.

Once again thrown away
swept and tossed from the chase
living elusive dreams
displayed before my face
Who were you, anyway?
Was it always about the need?

Yes, I remember still
ingrained in my soul
traces of you still visible
warnings trigger modes
you left your mark behind
lingering in the deeds

Kiera Miranda
Tucson, AZ United States

North to Alice

North to Alice, he went north—the rush was on.
Big Kev left Adelaide to go to Alice Springs;
He went in search for work you know, to see what life could bring.
He found a new excitement there, where his life became a dream.
He joined a cattle drive up north, just east of Alice Springs.

Big Kev drove the cattle, with the boys in the outback.
He took his blue heelers, and drove that cattle track.
Northern territory was his domain, where the dust is in the air;
And the barren land he travelled was wide, dry and bare.

The dingoes and kangaroos, they share this barren land.
The sound of hoofs, the dog's barking: Big Kev's in demand.
This dusty trail, this Aussie way, where the wildlife's not scarce—
Big Kev drove that cattle, across the wilderness.

Dry river beds he followed, till he came to a billabong
Where the swaggies all rested, told jokes and sang their songs.
But Big Kev had only one thing, that was on his mind...
To keep a movin' on that track, getting cattle stationed on time.

Sharon Seys
Goolwa, SA Australia

I live in a little place called Goolwa where the river Murray meets up with the sea. Sometimes writing a little poetry eases some of the stresses in everyday life. I like writing Australian lyrics to different pieces of music as I find this to be a challenge and quite interesting. This little town is full of beauty, which is surrounded by wildlife. Goolwa has abundant history, one of the Australian films, Storm Boy was created around Goolwa and the coorong—a peaceful place for writing poetry and other works.

Better

She waits for him to fall asleep, so she can lie awake and weep
Pain she feels is so unreal; she hasn't even had a correct meal
Coming home and feeling alone—desperate and hurting to the bone
She dreams of one day being happy, finding a relationship that's sappy
Being bullied all day long, cutting or burning she knows is wrong
She does it so that they can't hurt her; for doing it herself, she'd prefer
She feels like she is worthless, she knows her life is a mess
Each day she tries to be strong, but everything just feels so wrong
Her father doesn't even care. Her life it feels so unfair
When her father picks up that bottle, it's her neck that he will throttle
She'll scream and cry, and fight she'll try
Her mother never wanted to see...years before she hung on a tree
Bruises across her young flesh, a friend is to whom she'll confess
To everything that's happened, her funeral she's asked to attend
The girl says goodbye and walks back home; her friend, confused, sits
	alone
For she knew something was wrong, at home the girl turns on a song
Her father is still not there—these feelings are not ever rare
She'll miss her friend, she knows its true, but she's been feeling
	completely blue
She goes to the bathroom and takes the pills, for her pain is what really
	kills
She takes a handful and swallows, darkness and sickness soon quickly
	follow
She feels herself slipping away, hears sirens from far away
Somewhere, a distant voice appears; her friend discovers what she fears
An ambulance soon arrives, for her life it will soon strive
She's getting better day by day and owes her life to her friend, Fay
This girl survived, so can you find that strength that's within you
People care, they really do. Life gets better, even you know that's true

Desserra Small
Williston, VT United States

*This poem was inspired by friends and family. There are a lot of things that have
happened to people—teens I don't even know but still care about. I felt the need
to try and get this out to people all over, so they can help people, before it's too late.*

The Quarter Jar

It's been there for almost ten years now.
Every three or four months, it gets emptied—
but now, it's almost too full.
She was lying there, waiting for him to finish
so she could turn out the light,
when he came into the room.
Heard that for a quarter I could get
a little lovin' in here, he said.
How much will I get for two?
She laughed at his silly nonsense
and reached for the light.
Wow! Stopped her hand in mid-reach.
You're either really, really good or
you're really, really old he said,
Grinning and nodding toward the full jar.
She laughed again at his silly nonsense
and turned out the light,
all the while basking in the glow of his smile.
Do you come here often? He teased.
Only when the sum of the quarters offered
surpasses my age, she replied with a grin.
And he laughed as the quarters
slipped from his hand into
the mouth of the jar.

Renee Driscoll
Fort Collins, CO United States

The Fading Scent of Perfume

In the deepest memories of my mind,
There is a place to where I wish to go.
Remembering a woman fair and kind,
I miss her more than she will ever know.
And yet, I still find myself asking how
It is we could have passed each other by.
Although, I cannot think about that now—
She disappeared without a reason why.
The air is still, and she has gone away;
I sit and wonder where this woman went.
Hoping we meet again another day,
For each moment with her is time well spent.
Now, my tearful eyes scan this empty room,
That's filled with the fading scent of perfume.

Thomas Koron
Grand Rapids, MI United States

I was born in Grand Rapids, MI on May 19, 1977. I have attended Northview High School, Grand Rapids Community College, Aquinas College and Western Michigan University. I have always had a strong passion for poetry. I believe it is more than simply words written or printed on a page. Poetry is an actual living, breathing entity that can change our lives and elevate our spirits. It is capable of painting a vivid portrait of any subject, emotion or moment in time. These are the very elements of poetry that are truly immortal.

Day of the Sun

The day of the sun is mine in early morning
Trees whistle the song of light carried by the breeze
Luna wades the horizon longer than she should
and nobody minds her company
The sky lights up lavender and gold
People stop to smell the colors in the sky
Fog raises high to touch the red fire coming over the trees
A prayer is offered and sanctity resumes
The day of the sun is no longer mine
Early morn has faded into day

Dennis Allen
Cottondale, FL United States

I write poetry, parables, children stories, and short stories. My muse comes from life and things I have experienced. Life is tough right now; I am attempting to establish myself as a writer, and I am a full-time college student majoring in religious history. My works are about nature, spirituality, or life choices. My poetry is straight from my soul, and I leave nothing out.

Saddened

In memory of Brian Whitlock, Madison, GA.

today you plucked a beautiful rose from our life
he never had a chance to take a wife
our hearts are heavy, sadden and so blue
we can't believe this can be true
he was the sparkle in our eyes
you say to ask not so many whys
he was the best of the best
he stood out from the rest
his smile would light up anyone's day
he was everyone's friend in many a way
our life will never be the same
we wanted him to carry on our name
take care of him till we get there
we know he is in the best of care
we miss you, son
God said your work on earth was done

Patsy Hanson
Rutledge, GA United States

Heartbroken

Tears cannot explain the pain and emptiness that still remains
I lost the fight, but I cannot lose the war
I never knew how our love could be restored
I once said that I didn't need you
You were lame
But now I realize the pain without you is too much to tame
I cry and scream trying to escape the mistake I claim
Yet your hurt and my stupidity is to blame
I love you more than I love myself
Without you, I cannot be no one else
Our love is strong, this I know
But the feeling without you is too much for me to tow
My hopelessness is too much to disclose
My shadow being solo on the wall is too much for me to share
You know better than anyone how strong I am
But me without you is too much to bear

Deserae Cook
Spokane, WA United States

Writing poetry has always been in my life as far as I can remember. Poetry, for me, releases past and everyday troubles in my life. Reading and writing has a lot of importance to me. It helps me overcome obstacles I am going through at that certain point in my life. For example, "Heartbroken"—my longtime boyfriend and I split up and he moved back across the country. I was so depressed and distraught; I instantly went home and wrote this poem with tears in my eyes and sent it to him.

Love and Loss

It was a summer's eve so warm and bright
When her bountiful beauty caught my eye.
I then swooped in with the feeling so right;
I then fell for her, as she did for I.
We laughed and loved all summer's season long,
And were glowing in each others presence.
We drifted apart as summer went on,
Knowing each other only as peasants.
The feelings would still come up now and then,
But our glow had faded to a dim light;
I tried so hard to keep it going then,
Showering her with all my love and might.
But to no avail did these actions work,
Even though she told me they really did.
Breaking my heart by falling for a jerk,
Treating me far worse than a little kid.
Though the anger and sadness made me bawl,
I learned a lesson much greater than this...
A query by the best poet of all,
That did take me out of this dark abyss:
For is it better to have loved and lost,
Or better to have never loved at all?

Drew Stelling
Coto De Caza, CA United States

The Fall

He takes my hand to tell me the news,
but I can't feel his warm hand resting on mine.
My fingers twitch, but I can't feel them there. My hand is numb.

You have broken radius and ulna,
and your ulnar nerve is severely damaged.
The doctor with bright eyes looks upon my agonized face.
My bones are snapped. Not just fractured. Not just cracked.
Both are broken in half.

Each of his adjustments sends a shock through my arm,
as if I've grabbed an electric fence.
I lie down, hugging my arm to my chest. I cringe, teeth clenched.

My first thought—How will I play guitar?
The realization that I wouldn't be able to play
hurt more than the grinding of my bones scraping against one another.

My thoughts flash back to the stupidity that broke my arm.
I shouldn't have taken the dare. I made the kick. Both feet hung in the
    air,
right leg above my head. Falling back, with nothing I could do to stop
    the inevitable;
I landed on my left arm, and it gave with a snap.

At the memory of the moment of impact, I'm brought back to reality—
Back to the white walls of the hospital room.
The pain that shoots through my body catches me by surprise as I
    constrict.
I can't think back to that moment…
The moment when more than just my arm was suddenly shattered.
The moment when my whole life changed in an instant.
While viewing the scene, I again replay in my mind's eye,
I can do nothing but lay and cry.

Sasha Heikkila
Buxton, OR United States

Undesirable Love

Mixed emotions
Feeling confused
Sometimes feeling mistreated
And often used

The love so strong
Its hurts to think about letting go.
But afraid of the uncertainty
And afraid that it might show.

Never speaking of the truth,
Never wanting the conflict—
For everything she does is wrong,
And there would be no denying it.

The ring on her finger makes the statement, "the binding of love."

She gives and she gives,
With all of her heart;
And he drains her of all she has,
And it tears her apart.

She just wants to be happy.

Christine E. Pruett
Brighton, IL United States

Drowning

I dive off a cliff
and splash into the water
I'm holding my breath
trying to swim up
but its so dark
I can't tell
which way is up or down
and left or right
my lungs are tired
it feels like hours
I open my eyes
and all I see is darkness
my eyes start to sting
from the salty water
my lungs ache
and my head hurts
but something tells me
to keep my mouth shut
I try my hardest
but I have to give up
I take a breath in
and water fills my mouth
my lungs
I start to gasp for air
but I get water
my eyes sting worse
my head hurts
I close my eyes
and sink to the
cold ground
I just found down

Paige Lynn Landry
Maynard, MA United States

Change

Embrace the changes as they near,
Even if they bring chaos and fear.
If it was truly meant to be,
Then it will happen gradually.
By human nature we fear what we want
And tend to want what we fear
It's always at the forefront of our mind
And we dwell upon it from time to time,
We dwell upon it from time to time.
But when the changes come
It is not as bad as it appeared to be,
The fear it causes sends everything out of proportion.
Changes we experience balance out life,
Even if it only seems to make it wrong instead of right.
Eventually we accept what fate has handed us
And the chaos settles down
We learn to handle everything change throws at us,
We learn to live what it throws at us down.
Embrace the changes as the occur, don't shove them away
Embrace what life brings, live life to the fullest every day.

Christy Carter
Barstow, CA United States

Statistic

She never thought she'd become a statistic
She never thought it would happen to her
She never thought she'd get that bad
She never thought she'd go that far

She never realized what was happening
Until it was almost too late
She never realized how bad she was getting
Until it was almost too late

It had begun to consume her
It had begun to take over her life
It had begun to control her thoughts
It had begun to control her

She was ashamed
Of herself
She was sick
Of herself

She nearly became a statistic
She nearly lost it all
She nearly forgot everything she'd worked for
She nearly lost it all

She never thought she'd become a statistic
She never thought she'd get so close
She nearly became a statistic
But she caught herself

Shelby Ridenour
Mount Pleasant, IA United States

The Face of a Woman

She scolds the wind for blowing flowers away
Just when the show made her smile

You chiller of marrow
You bender of oaks in a storm
You carried my secret for a fly to the ends of the earth
Away went the grace that was oh, so the face of a woman

I long to kiss her
Kneeling in prayer I wish…I hope for that smile to appear
Can I tell you I love her?

Let time explain us
Her feelings join with mine
Leaving nothing behind
Secure in its place is this face of a woman

James Martin
Bristol, CT United States

My Inspiration

Be my inspiration
To write a poem
Something you can take
And keep at home
A way to smile
And feel some peace
And when you're stressed
To help it cease
Immortal words
Written and true
A poem is all about
From me to you
My thoughts on paper
Straight from the pen
They came from love
And Heaven above
May you find
Many peaceful times
From these verses
And meaningful rhymes
Thank you for you
Your inspirations too
For you're in my heart
Always, forever, and true.

Daniel Svoboda
Van Vleck, TX United States

Each day, I'd like to think we wake up refreshed and looking forward to seeing the day or night. The oak trees around here always seem to have leaves, and I love to see the green of the trees after a rain. I take time to notice the leaves and branches, and even blades of grass. There is so much we can use to make poetry and use for inspirations, but it's the people who help me smile—the cashiers, waitresses, coworkers. So here's one from me to all of you.

Do You Know Me?

I nudged you this morning to get you out of bed
So you wouldn't be late for work.
You looked at Me but didn't notice!
Cause you don't know Me.

I buckled up beside you and had to grab the wheel
You tried to text and spilled your coffee.
You looked at Me but didn't notice!
Cause you don't know Me.

I touched your shoulder when you hung your head
As your work day continued to get worse.
You looked at Me but didn't notice!
Cause you don't know Me.

I took your hand in mine as you sat crying
Feeling sad, alone and helpless.
You looked at Me but didn't notice!
Cause you don't know Me.

I lay beside you as you pulled the covers
over your head to sleep. You looked at Me but didn't notice!
'Cause you don't know Me.

But I know you; I know all of you
I know all of you by name
I know your wants, desires,
troubles, sorrows and pain
I know! Do you know Me?

Donna Carter
Franklinton, NC United States

For many years, I struggled with following my own plan. Then one day, I read some
words on a billboard in a church yard and realized I could not go on without the
right hand of Jesus. Once I followed God's plan, my life of struggles became bumps
in the road; and every day has become a possibility with many opportunities.

Don't Judge

Why do people have to judge
Everyone they see?

Height, size, looks, brains,
Even sexuality!

It's not nice, it's not fair
It is simply rude.

To judge anybody
With a system that is crude.

If you just give them a chance
Learn who they are really.

You may be shocked to find out
Your judgment was silly!

Mikayla Mehelich
Belfair, WA United States

Lord, I Promise…(Forgiveness)

Lord, I promise to release this stress
To relinquish this pressure upon my chest
To forgive them for the pain that had transpired
I don't want hell for them at their finest hour
We all are humans, we all have sin
But some of these battles we cannot win
Asking for forgiveness seems so far away
When we are fighting demons every day
Lord, I promise to let them enter
Not to be as cold as snow days of winter
High expectation is a setup for the fall
But low expectation can cripple us all
So tell me, who set the curve?
The ideal of forgiveness seem so secure
Forgiveness for me seems like an enemy
So that's when I give up and set them free
Lord, I promise to let them try
Because tomorrow, we all could die
Holding this on my soul wouldn't be right
To take it with me once I take flight
What if the angels told me I had to go?
Then the demons told me it is a hell no
So then my soul would be stuck in limbo
I forgive you, brothers, I'm letting it go!

Nicholas Edwards
Ames, IA United States

Growing up on the South Side of Chicago with no father around, a mother struggling to raise five boys, and living in an area with gangs, knowledge was my way to a better life. Sadly, being smart meant that you were better than the next. Although I didn't believe that, it didn't stop some family and childhood friends from ignorance. As I mature, I learn to forgive and help those who believe there is more to life than "the hood." Now being on Youtube.com as SincereNick, I'm truly here to "help you out." No matter what life throws at you, my motto to all is to "stay positive."

Battlefield

Listen to the sounds of peace and quiet in the air,
Eyes closed and arms resting by the sides.
Relief of surviving another day can smelled miles away;
The battlefield is dangerous grounds.
But, there is so much joy, there are also
Hard times, hard knocks, hard heads;
it's all a part of the daily routine,
Trying desperately to convince others to dream.

It seems that a losing battle is ahead
But determination keeps one grounded.
It's a twenty-four-hour job: dirty work, grind.
What's the reward? Little recognition, even smaller pay,
and little personal time.

The money isn't everything—if it was,
Who would dare enter these treacherous grounds?
Smiles, thank you, and "Good Morning, Mr. or Ms."
Keeps the soldiers from losing their minds.
It's all in the life of a teacher!

Rakesha Jones
Robinsonville, MS United States

*I am a middle school math teacher who fell in love with poetry when I was in the
sixth grade. It is one of my favorite hobbies and a way to express myself.*

This Is Me Now

Shadows on those four walls surrounded me
Who I was, who I wanted to be

I was not who you saw
I was not who you thought

You all said I was so lucky
So skinny and sweet

No one knew it was because I didn't eat
projecting perfection, secretly hating my reflection

One step closer to my death
every bite I declined
a part of the vibrant me died

Pedaling mile after mile
feeling weak, but I knew I couldn't stop
for I was just not small enough

This goal was unreachable, unattainable
I wanted so badly just to die

Very few asked if I was ever okay
that was just another day

That was the old me
this is me now

Sometimes I go back to those days of doubt
turning myself inside out
I may never be perfect, but I'll always strive

I'm learning more than ever before
I'm learning to grow
instead of only want more

Holly Damron
New London, OH United States

Forever Love

Your love came in and filled my heart
I knew this love would be
My one true love my heart was sure
The last I'd ever see
As years went by our lives were changed
We slowly grew apart
But one thing stayed down deep inside
Your love locked in my heart
We drift away then back again
I guess life's cruel that way
But through it all your soft sweet love
Inside my heart has stayed
The day draws near I feel the pain
I know the time is close
When I must say goodbye again
To the one I've loved the most
I pray somehow our lives will find
A place where we can be
Together again your hand in mine
For all eternity

Larry Lusk
Palestine, TX United States

I think I inherited my poetic interests from my mother; she loved poetry and loved writing. Most of the things I write about have been inspired by events in my life. Some happy moments inspired happy poems, and difficult times inspired more deep and serious feelings to come out. I guess if I went through all the things I have written, it would show a pretty good timeline of the ups and downs of my life.

It Just Has Not Really Been a Funny Day to Me

It just has not really been a funny
day to me.

Why is it that just now, of all days,

my dog just ran away?
You see, this morning, it was truly a

beautiful, clear, sunny day;
I could not wait to take my dog to the

park for some play.
But that's not why I now feel so sad

today,
as I watch my dog run and play.
Nor is it just that he just ran away, on

this spectacularly
sunny day.
Some may ask why I am so sad on this

beautiful day.

Michael Diehl
Anaheim, CA United States

Disappointment

She closes her eyes full of sorrow;
In her chest, a deep sadness,
On her lips, a horrid sigh.
She entails a silent limp to her every step,
Which she takes note of, then discards it.
In her mind she waits for everything to settle—
Yet, this time could be occupied elsewhere.
Her heavy lashes beat similar to her melancholy heart,
Her temple, a protesting throng of worry.
Her every breath is so tasteless, so hollow.
She prays it won't be this way much further in time;
For by day, she dies a little more inside.
She meddles for a truth in another body other than man,
Yet she feels so empty deep within.
She hears nothing—the silence echoes against her desolation.
Her fingers grasp the droplets wrung from her innermost core:
They fall so blissfully upon her face.
She longs to feel loved again, like she was once shown.
She finds herself in these states more often when alone at night.

Yet she stands, smiles, wipes the sadness from her being,
and braces herself for another disappointment.

Her name is, "Woman."

Tessa Marie High
Santee, SC United States

My Eyes Have Been Opened

My eyes have been opened so I can see the light
It is time for me to begin the fight
I must not let Satan win another round
for the results would be my soul eternally bound
The fight is real and very prevalent today
and Satan is looking for souls with him to stay
The only chance I will have to win
is by letting go of all of my sins
By pleading with my Heavenly Father for the light
and giving me the strength to win the fight
It is so easy to allow my thoughts to be clouded
and my hopes and desires to all be rerouted
It is sometimes so hard to let go of all of my sins
but I have to let go to allow my heart to mend
Satan is working every minute of each day
clouding my thoughts and saying I don't need to pray
But when I read the scriptures, ponder and pray
the clouds are lifted and my life doesn't seem so gray
Then I am inspired to do what is right
and now, like Moroni, I can win the fight
Or become like Abinadi and a warning I will give
to start doing what is right, so in Heaven we can live
or to be as Ammon and share God's love
so all may some day get to live up above

Roger Barker
Providence, UT United States

*I love to write poetry, and I hope someday my poems will truly touch the hearts of
many people and give them a strong desire to be kind and thoughtful to others—
or make someone happy and feel good about themselves.*

Unnoticed

In the corner
Of the room.
Invisible to most,
Unnoticed by many.
This is me,
Thinking about
If I was noticed,
Would I be a different person?
Would I be
Liked and loved by more?
Would my mistakes
Be more noticed as well?
In the corner,
Of the room.
Invisible to most,
Unnoticed by many.
This is me,
Thinking.

April Simpson
Garland, TX United States

Gothic Soul

There is no real way
to say what I wish.
I have had a wondrous foray
of dancing in the night mist.

My body was weightless
in the midnight sky.
My mind was restless
in the fanatic's eye.

My soul dances to a tune
of mythical energies.
Dark images cause my swoon
in an entanglement of enemies.

I love the night
and creatures of the dark.
I forsake the light
and all my species' bark.

My dreams are here
within my lover's embrace.
My soul is near
so do not fear.

I am happy within
this dark embrace.

Maura Neland
Briceville, TN United States

I am a twenty-two-year-old who lives in Briceville, TN. I love to read and am a goth by choice. I also love to cosplay and have become a regular of the Middle Tennessee Anime Convention.

Linger

Melancholy waltzes in
dangerous and seductive
it caresses me intimately
like the lover it proposes
to be. Cold lips cover mine
stealing breath, I cannot
find my way to the air
beyond its cloying scent.
One and then another
of my feeble defenses
fails. I fall deeply into
its dark embrace.
I allow it to roam
my body, take my
soul and caress
my mind—completely
lost, found
dark and soft, so
easy, so overwhelming
nothing to break through
but a faint light…no just
a thought and then
my lover's embrace
takes over again
and again—restless, relentless

Tiffany Bunge
Lansing, MI United States

I am the mother of two beautiful teenage daughters and a full-time educator as well as a PhD candidate at Michigan State University. My poetry is predominantly an exorcism of personal demons and falls between the areas of satirical commentary reflective in tone. Poetry simply happens—almost a force unto itself for me. I hope that readers connect to my work on some universally true level, that as humans we all experience the same emotions and searches, although our responses to life and choices may vary.

Beloved Mortal (David Clay)

Before I ever saw you, I loved you—more than I can express
When you were born, I knew the true meaning of happiness
Big and strong and healthy; your first expression, a smile
Even your first photo reflected a certain special style
Your gentle spirit always came through as you grew in body and mind
Becoming a very handsome young man, with a heart so loving and kind
Sometimes melancholy, oft times wayward too
Shying away from convention, defending your right to be you
A certain mischievous streak of rebellion: "To thine own self be true"
Words that, early on, became a way of life to you
I admire your passion for life, making each day seem brand new
Good or bad, lived to the fullest, daring to be you
Today and always, I hope you see
Precious, only son, you mean the world to me

Carolyn Maddon
Shingletown, CA United States

I am a retired Native American woman who expresses my thoughts and feelings and past experiences with poetry. I have written thirty or forty poems and continue to find peace and joy in the written expression. Writing is also cathartic for me during times of sorrow.

Ego's Molded Way

The symbols that we choose today
To mark the ego's path
Are often foolish, sometimes prized,
Yet surge from wellspring's wrath:

The tattooed snake on arm devised
Repelling parent's touch;
The nickname shouted to the world
Defining soul as such;

The face we think stands there unfurled
With hidden self secured;
And then the scheme to make it true
The outer shell preferred!

It's all a game for public view,
The lie created play—
The acts, the scenes, with craft fought through
For ego's molded way.

And is reality our own?
Or has some force within us grown
That makes self pawn that must engage
Strange animations on life's stage?

John Gilbert Fuller
Warrenville, IL United States

John Gilbert Fuller was born in Indianapolis, IN. He received a BA from Brown University and attended JD Northwestern University Law School. John is the author of novels: Portrait of a Boy, The Forest Holds a Secret Place *and* A Poet's Alchemy. *John also authored the award-winning short story, "Emma Has Her Way." He is also a published contributor over the years to a multitude of poetry publications.*

Prayer Mail

Somewhere in the emptiness of the mailbox
and the silence of the telephone
Are thoughts of you and memories of our friendship;
They make me laugh and smile when my heart is heavy
with the world's care.

I know that life has taken us down different roads
that keeps us fairly busy.
It's for that reason I try to
make my thoughts into little prayers,
Because I know that God is always with you—
in the midst of your cares.

So, when the phone is not ringing
and the mailbox is empty,
Remember I'm sending you my love
on a wing and a prayer.

Genelle H. Powell
Birmingham, AL United States

A Posteriori

The only faith that I keep
Is in the tip
Of your razor blade
And the words that it makes
Me bleed.
But, really, you're all the same;
Permanent or temporary,
Just another void with a name.
And a muse hidden
Within my veins.

Gaylen Cook
Duncannon, PA United States

I've been writing (or attempting to) since I can remember. Relationships and love have been the biggest influences on my writings. "A Posteriori" is no exception. Titled after the philosophical phrase for "from experience" in Latin, this piece represents some of the relationships that I've been through. They've been good and bad, but they've been learning experiences and bottomless pods of inspiration.

Tempting Ideas

Dedicated to my wonderful sister Willy

These tempting, unforgettable ideas—they hold and express feelings
and emotions, or even a state of being.
They become happy, sad, angry, depressing, dark, emotionless,
joy, encouraging, outgoing, personal, secretive, coded, known to all,
and much, much more. But all I know is it is worth getting it out.
It flows: from your brain to your heart, then to your hand onto the
    lead tip
of your pencil onto the paper or to your fingertips on to the keyboard.
But all that I really, truly know, is that it is a burst of energy
just waiting to be released.

Sara Duquette
Sioux City, IA United States

Broken Poets

Blame my liver, shame my soul;
Fame my pain, and settle your score.
Because I'm not a killer, I'm never with malice—
Always there for everyone, raising the chalice.
For the years I ignored and continued with play,
Poisoned by the venom which led my path astray.
My policy of honesty was corrupted,
And yet, my heart was there—
Drowned by the misery when others couldn't care.
So time bared my closest shave.
Who's to blame
If I'm the soldier KIA on tracks before the train?
Forever then shamed!
With intention comes vibed inception...
Marriage, pain, kids, complexities,
barrages, stains, friends, agonies!
So f*ck it if I can't treasure my name;
My selfless acts seemed only to grind against the grain.
I'm a paneless window who tries to shield the rain.
I was the best friend you ever had, surely still am,
But if building the bridge is a burden, I'd rather the banner across it ran.
If silence is golden for my mind exposed,
I'll think away thoughtlessly, selfishly—
Is this what you so wish?
Are we capiche? Comprende?
Then look what we created, friend. Here's my good intention.

John Rossiter
Chessington, Surrey United Kingdom

My life is an awakening—understanding my errors in what I may do and the problems faced, the traumas felt, one can only use it as an armory of knowledge. With this, my poetry through the music that suits my mood at the time summons ideas, inspirations and aspirations to exorcise my demons. I'm far from religious, but very spiritual. I'm far from profiting from life, but I understand my purpose. Life is about experience and leaving behind your name as a legacy.

Free

Daughters of the moon
Sons of the wind
Children of the earth
We are all one
We live first among
The trees
Then out fellow brothers
And sisters
We live not among the
Buildings of brick
And estranged wires
Mother Nature bore us
To fly from our
Barbaric tree stands

Cierra Merryman
Westminster, MD United States

I started writing poetry during a difficult time in my life, and honestly, I believe that poetry saved my life. Now, poetry is a great passion of mine.

Where Are You?

February 2012

Where are you?

In the deep recesses of my heart
Echoing the depths of a true, unending love
You will always be there, locked forever
Soul mates we will be together as ever.

February 18 2012

Lost
Lost in the soft twilight
A sweet person, reaching out for help
recalling memories of a love so true
forlorn, facing the unknown
hoping to return some day
in the spring of hope.

Caring Santos
Sarasota, FL United States

I write poems when I am sad or experiencing a loss.

Daddy's Girl

I will always be Daddy's girl
Dad would be there when I had fallen down
He would pick me up when I got hurt
I will always be Daddy's little girl
He would take me out on the motorcycle
He was there to take care of me when I was sick
I will always be Daddy's little girl
Dad always brought me to church
He would love me no matter what I've done
I will always be Daddy's little girl

Amanda Young
Breckenridge, MN United States

Party Fit for a Rock Star

It all started with a simple birthday getaway…
In late September we said goodbye to Philly and climbed aboard the
    Majesty.
Bermuda, are you ready for us? We're on our way.
My birthday came around, and I was surprised with a party.

The best part was when the crowd erupted in a sweet serenade.
I went to bed that night feeling like a super star.
Little did I know, that was just the start of an eventful parade!
It was strange waking up the next morning and not being able to go
anywhere without people—
especially little kids—knowing who you are.

During the rest of the trip, people would want to hang out with me, ask
for a picture, or want to know if I'd be at the parties and dance.
Not a day went by where I didn't find myself on the ship TV.
I even found myself a little romance.
I never dreamed that I'd be the topic of the paparazzi.

The party never ended.
I will never forget the year when I turned twenty-three.
I still keep in touch with the people I befriended,
They mean so much to me.

Abigail Hucker
Chester, PA United States

Halloween Tonight

Trick or treat, smell my feet
Is something we used to say
But this is more than scary, it's Halloween today
Ghouls and ghosts that haunt the sky
Witches with black cauldrons
An orange moon that dots the sky
Black cats that look you in the eye, it's Halloween tonight
So frightful and delightful, and Oh! How scary
We shriek at every sound—boy, do our voices carry
For this is more then an adventure that lurks in the night
And, oh! What a fright, as we cringe at every sight
At all the things that we hear
And go bump in the middle of the night
With its hidden surprises behind every gate
We don't know what to do; oh boy, how we shake
For this is Halloween's dance of a spirited night
Of frightening sounds, of shaking and dragging of chains
Boos and shrill screeching, reaching our ears along the way
And as we reach every door, we wait with anticipation
See what treats we'll receive or of tricks of anticipation
For this is Halloween tonight

Pamela Ward
Monrovia, CA United States

Peace

Deep and profound yet so hard to attain
Why do so many people take this in vain?
If this would be everybody's concern
This would be a better place to live in.

Too much clutter and disorganized things
War and hatred here, there and everywhere
Why don't we clean up and stop making mess
Tidy thoughts lead to an organized world.

Things spic and span, kind words to everyone
Clean surroundings, a smile, a lending hand
Let's start from ourselves, not blame anyone
Peace will be attained—sure, it will be grand!

Juvy Mangulabnan
Garden City, KS United States

I write poems as a hobby. It is my way of expressing my thoughts and feelings for the moment. I usually do it for special people as a sign of appreciation—to show how much I treasure them. I also write about things I am passionate about. Furthermore, I write poems to inspire, and I hope they serve as instruments to create change and make this world a much more wonderful place in which to live.

Who Is That Man?

There's a suspicious stranger following me.
He's secretive and sly and not easy to see.
He's there, wherever I go
His reflection is in every window and mirror
anywhere I happen to be

He looks like a relative,
for he has some resemblance to me
but he's old and haggard and obviously
senior to me
By his grimace I can tell he resents my handsome,
good-looking, youthful appearance

When I look at him, I have a sense of satisfaction
happy that I persist as that young man
I have always been and continue to be

but it's definitely disturbing
I find him there every morning
I glance in the mirror and there he is staring at me
when all I want is just to comb my hair

I only wish he'd move out of the way and let me see
that true handsome, good-looking youthful,
reflection of *me*

Allen Tilden
Albuquerque, NM United States

Rainbow

Bleeding waves crash onto the sandy shores
As the stars sing sweet songs of allure,
Raindrops descend from unknown heavens
Trickling from head to toe
And calming the rigid souls,
The stars align for this beautiful sight
Illuminates the mystery in the world
Faces collide and dangerously dance
The rhythms of a beating heart
Yet I wonder
Day after day
Why the moon does not speak
And why the symphonies do
Not play within the wonders of the world
Dreaming and gazing
Curiously questioning
Why does the rainbow shine?

Gabrielle Catalano
Carlsbad, CA United States

Poetry is beautiful—not because it's a form of self-expression, but because it speaks in ways we can't. I don't think when I'm writing poetry; I just let my mind go free. I hope to be a creative writing teacher one day, and possibly a writer and a poet.

The Wolf Within

This is how the story goes
Of the lone wolf
Who no one had ever really known
Until she finally stood

I wandered from pack to pack
Needing somewhere to belong
But all of them would say, "Stay back!"
When I howled my mournful song

Of the wolves that would get near me
They would always call me names
Tearing me down, piece by piece
To break me was their aim

Then came the day I stood my ground
They still tried to act so tough
But I would not back down
That still didn't make them give up

The battle was so hard and long
I thought the bell of my death would surely toll
But a voice deep inside me said,
"Don't give up, lone wolf, your claws have not yet dulled!"

So loud enough for others to hear
I howled of the battle I'd won
Then came a pack of kind wolves that said, "It's okay, lone wolf, we're
here.
Never again will you be alone."

Shelbie Hale
Lexington, IN United States

Who, What, Where, When and Why

Who started it all?
The destruction and world's downfall

What can all of us do?
Someone must have the right clue

Where did it all go wrong?
It's been going on, far too long

When did it all start?
This world is falling apart

Why so many wars
For so many shores?

Questions to think about
Let's all, everyone, stand up and shout
We all have to get it right
Clean up this earth, hold on tight
Because right now...
We all are in for the fight...
For our lives

Phyllis Ketchum-Greenwalt
Sarasota, FL United States

The Mist

Upon awakening to the start of a new day,
not wanting to face the strife of the new way,
it hits me head on, and all fades away, it's the mist.

By midday the grey returns, and the body and mind
become numb at these times questionable traits,
but in an instant the grey vanishes,
for in the mind's memory stands the mist.

At late afternoon the rush begins,
attempting to accomplish another days feat,
tired and weary, oh how I long for retreat,
wrapped in the warmth of the mist.

When evening's shadow unfolds, I can hardly wait,
the thought consumes me, it rejuvenates my soul,
for soon it will be time to be embraced once again by the mist.

It's my shelter from the storm, its rapture makes me whole, complete,
and at peace with the world, it warms me from the inside out,
it's my mother for her guidance, it's my children for the laughter,
and teaching me the new way, it's my husband for showing me
dreams can become reality, they are the mist.

Peggy Simoneaux
Liberty, MS United States

Ice-Cold Hands

I'm going to sit in the rain
Wash all my tears away
The drops taking the pain
Why must I feel this way?
I feel my grip loosen
Reality slipping from my fingertips
Falling deeper in the darkness I'm in
Ice-cold hands pull at my hips
The rain taking my hurt
Darkness closing in
The tears on my face leave scars that are burnt
My strand of life is getting thin
Ice-cold hands pull once more
My body gives in
Fall short, never learning what life was for
Ice-cold hands finally win
I sat in the rain
To wash all my tears away
I thought the drops would take the pain
I know why I felt that way
Meant to dwell in the ice-cold land
When I was taken that day
The ice-cold and I, hand in hand
The day the rain took the pain away

Trina Olson
Carson City, NV United States

The Sweetness of Love

Love is more than a magical feeling or a series of chemical reactions—
There's so much more involved than just physical attraction.
Yes, you can feel it in the rhythmic palpitations of your heart,
It's felt as your pulse races and butterflies in your belly begin to dart.
But, Love is a verb chock-full of tangibility...
Love is a destination, a place that's both beautiful and awe-inspiring.
Love has no time limitations; there are no chronologic boundaries;
Love has a way of making a few moments feel like an eternity.
Real love has a sweetness that seems to saturate the soul—
It's in the kindness of our words, and it is clear in the actions we show.
It's expressed in the marathon conversations that begin at ten at night
and go on and on quietly, until the morning light.
Love is in the sound of laughter, it's the light behind small smiles.
It's the feeling you get when you realize all life's pain was worthwhile.
Yet, it's still more than a feeling: it's a journey, it's time invested,
It's the result of a relationship that's been tried and tested.
You can see the proof of its existence in elderly couples holding hands.
We visualize it in hearts with arrows through them drawn in the sand.
It's the state of adoration you're in when you're in each other's
    presence—
That euphoric place you go when you're lost in each other's essence.
Love has an incontestable power, presence, and language all its own;
It's so omnipresent that no matter where you are, you're never truly
    alone.
Love is making time when there don't seem to be enough hours in the
    day,
And the sweetness of love speaks when we as people run out of words
    to say.

Tanika Barnett
Jacksonville, FL United States

If You Hoard Love

If you hoard love, it melts away. If you lock love, it breaks free
If you grab onto love, you end up holding an illusion
When you let love flower in its own way, it stays to support you
When you pass on love, it multiplies beyond measure
Doubt holds you landlocked in paralysis, unable to move either way
The time you spent or spend doubting is the time you are not alive
So rid yourself of the doubts and take that step, one way or another
Your heart knows what is best and so does God; so take it, right now
We get overwhelmed with the detail and complexities of life at times
Sometimes, we need some help to get untangled, to gain perspective
Help may come in human or divine form—it may be seen or unseen
So when it is all done and over with, if you find yourself
In a strange situation and can't understand what is happening just
Know you are feeling the emotions from hoarding love and all that
comes with it, so don't hoard a great gift from God, which is love
Just let go and live freely, but faithfully

Kenneth Brown
Killeen, TX United States

I am thirty-five years old and I'm from New Albany, MS. I am currently in the military and have been for over fifteen years now. I love to play sports, read and study the Bible, draw and write poems. My poetry comes from my life experiences and from the things I have seen in life. I want to write a book one day on life and love; that is my goal. I plan to go back to school and get my BA soon, and I look forward to getting started on my book.

Healing Waters

Healing waters are flowing to you
overflowing in grace to you
My love runs deep
my love runs wide
I give to you in unlimited supply
My love is flowing and pouring over you
I'm pouring in my oil and healing you
In this place there is healing love
Love is flowing deep and wide
it's pouring deep inside of you
In my love you are being healed

Sarah Roy
Roanoke, TX United States

I have been married to a wonderful man, Glen, for thirteen years. We have three amazing children: Isaac, Elisha, and Joshua. We live in Roanoke, TX. When I wrote this poem, I wanted to bring love and encouragement to many needing healing and to bless you and say, God loves you!

Natural Beauty

The flower's natural beauty brings to life in its creation
a purpose to our lives: to inspire, within our spirits,
a place where happiness, love, and dreams grow,
to inspire in each of us a passion to live his word.

The flower's natural beauty brings to life,
in its delicate existence,
a sense of protection that within
provides a warm flowing glow of trust in my heart
that all will be fine.

The flower's natural beauty brings to life a sense of uniqueness,
a sense of knowing that I too have been created for a purpose in
touching other's lives—to inspire a change in a world full of sin,
knowing that He, in creating my life, had a purpose, a plan,
and that He gave me my own natural beauty.

A beauty of faith that He, God, wants me!

Darla Beamon
Fresno, CA United States

I am a daughter, wife, mother, and grandmother. I have been married twenty-six years and have four wonderful children. Among the four, I have nine grandchildren. I am a retired teacher and love having more time to be creative. I love writing in general, but writing poetry calms me. I enjoy writing poems that make the reader think. I hope to spend a lot of time with my grandchildren; and when not with them, I want to write and create.

Human Art Show

Paint on your smile
Sculpt your body how people want to see you
Put yourself on display
Lay the brushes down, show the colors that are yours
How do you feel?
Like an art show
Move your arm it should be over there
That's better
That color should be darker
Put more rose here
How do you feel?
Like an art show
Paint
Paint
Paint
We paint ourselves on how people want to see us
Letting others paint our masterpiece,
How we look
How we feel
How we act
When will the painting stop?
When will the masterpieces be our own?
When will others stop mixing their colors with mine?

Corin Hale
Columbus, OH United States

Time Will Heal Your Pain

I remember when we were younger, how you always cared for me
or every time that I got hurt—you'd bandage all my bleeds
You always made sure that I ate well and the cloths I was wearing were
    straight
As I got older and got a job, you would call me so I wouldn't be late
You tutored me when it was needed in some of my school-year days
Thanks to you, it's helped me through; so, you deserved all of the praise
When I got older and moved on and the miles put us apart
my love for you was always so strong—you were always close to my
    heart
But our lives, as we know, are so very short; and I'm no longer here
    with you
The memories you carry of me, dear Baji, will continue to help you get
    through
As for each new day that passes your way and you see yourself starting
    to cry
just remember, my wonderful sister, you can always look up in the sky
and know that I'll always be with you, just not in the presence of your
    face
I'm much higher up in Heaven now, and it's such a beautiful place
So please, no longer mourn for me as time will heal your pain
Please know how much I loved you, dear Baji, and one day we'll be
    together again

Christine Stanbery
Wonder Lake, IL United States

"Time Will Heal Your Pain" was written for a colleague of mine, whose brother-in-law was killed in a random shooting in Afghanistan. His wife having a difficult time accepting the passing of her brother is what inspired me to write this poem as if he were speaking to her from Heaven. As we know, losing anyone is a terrible tragedy, and time usually helps ease the pain of a grieving heart. So reading anything inspirational always helps you remember happy memories and leaves your heart feeling better, as it does for me.

Untitled

Our hearts are the most interesting things we possess
Not just that they keep us alive
They express the words that the head cannot
When we are happy, they become light enough to soar on cloud nine
They beat ecstatically when that special someone is nearby
They are burdened with guilt when we make a big mistake
They are fragile enough for a sharp insult to break
They are brave when we choose to trust again
Our hearts are like a big house inviting loved ones in
They are sick with grief when we have to say our last goodbye in tears
They treasure our hope for blue sky when the storm clears
Our hearts are what keep our spirits forever young
One day we will leave this world behind and ascend to Heaven
And the only thing we can give to holy angels is our hearts
Our hearts mean so much more to us than we can imagine

Janeli Holladay
Fremont, CA United States

A Time of Wandering and Wondering

He flits from place to place
Testing the waters
And he wonders
Will I be welcome here
Or will I move on?
His backpack is loaded
Beyond its capacity
His back strains
As he picks it up again
And he wonders
Where will I sleep tonight?
The shadows deepen
The night stirs
Paces quicken
The heart pounds
Footsteps
Closer
The wandering begins again
And he wonders
Will I
Ever rest again?

Lee Hedstrom
Minneapolis, MN United States

Today

Today I extinguish
the candles lit
'cause nothing remains
it becomes a myth

Today, the blazing sun
will try again
to torch a world
"Hell, who's to blame?"

Today a lurking shadow
will regain its strength
for every move
N' every step
it'll have no end

Today a floating breeze
will brush away
the fallen leaves

Today, the hopes of life
will either expand
or drown
for every darkness
a speck of light
comes with a sound...

Serwat Chandna
Mississauga, ON Canada

Poetry is the language of a soul...

Our Heroes—Our Fathers

The men that were—our heroes
The men we called—our fathers
Worked hard to give us a better life
Than the ones that they were offered

Be honest, kind and respect your elders
Were important things they have taught us
Plus those lectures we heard more than once
We now teach our sons and daughters

Who knows why they have left us?
We just know they've gone away
But their memories we keep alive
In our hearts, they'll always stay

So it's up to us to go on in life
Become the best that we can be
Make them proud reach for the sky
Live the life for us they had dreamed

And when the darkest grief has lifted
We will remember: our lives were gifted
With the men we called our heroes
With the men that were—our fathers

Suzan Lewis-Escalona
Torrance, CA Romania

Dreamer

It's hot, and it's bright; a soft breeze fills the air
The waves crash, and gulls sing as the wind blows my hair
Summer is about freedom and laughter
No worries or qualms from here on after
The view from my perch is calming and sweet
I love the feeling of sand beneath my feet
The water, like crystals, glistens in the sun
While surfers and children splash, having fun
I pull off my Ray Bans and glance at you
You're tanning and golden because you love it here too
Standing I stretch, your eyes on me, so look back and set down my hat
You smile and chuckle; I love it when you do that
My hand reaches out and you take it fast
We both wish today could somehow last
Together, we walk to the edge of the world
You whisper you love me and call me your girl
The sun starts to set, the beach-goers leave
But we stay until dark, with our hearts on our sleeves
Then when we do go, you take me home and leave with a kiss
For certain, it will be you that I miss
To bed I go with an awed smile
Who would have known you'd steal my heart all the while?
Just as my eyes close and I fall into sleep
I am jarred into wakefulness as my neighbor's alarm beeps
My eyes scan the room and realize it was all a sweet dream
But I smile anyway—being a dreamer isn't as bad as it would seem

Raeanne Rankin
Carmichaels, PA United States

Untitled

I wrote your name on a piece of paper, but it blew away.
I wrote your name on my hand, but it washed away.
I wrote your name in the sand, but the waves whisked it away.
I wrote your name on my heart, and forever it will stay.

McKayla Ingram
Double Springs, AL United States

Say Goodbye

If I shall pass away on this very day
Do not cry
For I have cried enough for all of us
In this life
Do not hurt
For I have felt enough pain for the both of us
Do not forget
For I cannot forget you and the love, memories
That kept me alive, but
Do love with an open heart
Do cry with joy
Do live a full life
Until we meet again

Terese Marcoe
Republic, WA United States

A Man Alone...

I am a man—just a man—a man so alone...
With four walls in an empty house I call my home
Not even a woman here, I can call my own.

Some say, I'm "lucky to be free."
Women to love—not one—maybe as many as three.
If you like, sit in this room; then look at me.
Four walls in an empty house, I'm learning to call home.
Not even a woman for my very own.

Enjoy the loving you had, both you and she
Keep your memories locked in your hearts like they should be
Or the chances are, you will end up like me.
A single man—just a man—a man that became alone.
Confronted by four walls, in an empty house
Someone calls home.

You weigh what I say to be right or wrong
For I say what I feel; these thoughts are my own.
They come from secret parts of me I have never shown.
By now you must know why
I am that man—
Just a man—
A man alone...

Robert Garcia
King City, CA United States

The Walk

A flower, a building and a tree
These things are what I see
As I walk down the block
And kick a rock
and indulge in a playful immaturity
The scent of nature fills the air
But others start to hustle by checking their watches
And obviously don't care
Don't they notice? Don't they see?
Around them a natural beauty
I might just travel down the sidewalk
And hear the noises of squawking and talk
But people are people, wherever they're found
Like cars that roam our present ground
As I spot a man who litters a can
Beside a rusty fence
My eyes suddenly seem dense
With the fume of smoke
I hack and choke
And utter bitterly
As I see a bee pollinate a flower
I think I've had enough of this journey
I feel so sick and worried
Who cares about nature? Who needs this grass?
I think I'll just sit indoors instead

Fabiola Radosav
Elmhurst, NY United States

I've always loved poetry. My grandmother used to write poetry, but passed away of cancer a few years ago. She wrote many poems for me, so I'd like to carry on her tradition. I live in Elmhurst and I go to Leonardo Da Vinci Intermediate School; I am currently in seventh grade. I consider myself a very athletic person, and even though my favorite subject in school is science, I find ways to keep my passion for poetry alive. My poems are inspired by what I observe and perceive all around me. Nothing leaves me indifferent.

Forest of Tricks

Into the night where the darkness is thick
Into the mist to the forest of tricks
To dance with the ravens and call to the crows
Dance to the field covered with snow
The ritual begins soon, the tribute long due
Say farewell to those you knew
The night is alive, the birds are waiting
The demon himself is patiently debating
A servant to the song of the night
Priestess of the ritual has begun to recite
The innocent are safe behind their wall
But the wicked cannot help but answer the call

Anna Manley
Headland, AL United States

The Separation

You may be far from this breathing pulsation of mine
Yet, I cherish to behold in sincerity
my most Beloved sublime; I may no longer hold you
nor feel the silken velvet of your aging grace
yet the signature of your inner most rawness
bestows itself as the satin sheets of gentleness
upon the quivering of my inner space
Permeating your essence ashore the veils of
my reluctant days and open nightly doors
awaiting a flicker of thy glimmer in a dream
Eyes shut to feel the beauty of your kisses laced
upon the shedding of such mourning's shaky race
of my ticker's chase. Meandering through
the silts of drunken time
down on my begging tares of attachment I succumb
On my begging, aching knees, I hum
a softened, glistening dew of attempted self-soothing
lullaby of poetic repents, I rhyme
"For Goodness sake," I plead now and many thence
Liberate all that is not the crown of revelations
realized to be my own chosen reflections prized
Spread me wide as the seeds of awakening sown.
Hence, I seek my own chase to see and be seen as the Holiness
lured through my own mystical embrace
May the supremacy of gratitude be our rivers delight
and our soul's aspirations—the dawn of all light!

Tannauz Rahimpour
Victoria, BC Canada

This poem was inspired by the loss of the deepest love in my life. I have no formal education and find poetry to be the main way of modulating the intensity of my passionate heart and sensitive nature. "In creative expression, we find our deepest voice, and our souls calling to hence rejoice!" Thank you for hearing my aching voice!

Home

If home were anywhere
Where would I be?
Would I be in a house?
Or beside the windswept sea?
Would I open up my doors
To the darkest form of night?
Would I willingly give it up?
Or would I stand and fight?
If I had the choice today
To overthrow my fate,
Would I go to my death
If I knew it was too late?
Is there a home for me
Where I feel free and wanted?
Is there a life for me
Where my memories aren't haunted?
If I could have a home
It wouldn't be on earth.
I'd work toward my goal
And find my own self worth.

Wynter Harms
Blackburn, MO United States

God's Love

Our life is a rock in which God holds,
In whom He made us different from each mold.
His love gave us strength to go through anything,
Gave us a voice to rejoice and sing.
His Son's death gave us life to live;
It's up to us to learn to forgive.
We do have Him to call upon,
That's why He gave us His only Son.
He doesn't give us too much to handle,
He's there like a light from a candle.
As the whistle of the wind,
you hear His voice amend.
He sends us His drops of tears,
To take away all our fears.
It's God's love that makes us,
So, please don't make a fuss.
When it's time for us to go,
He will give us a beautiful show.
He sends us a sign with His white, snowy doves,
So, remember that it's all God's love.

Robin Howell
Memphis, TN United States

My Daddy

Bars and glass between us, you never did change
Like you said you would when I was younger.
Whether the bars be metal, or have the guys and a beer
Looking at you through the glass just causes more of my tears.

If I wasn't a strong-willed person, I would be broken into a million
    pieces
There were things left unspoken, that maybe I should have told you
I told you that I loved you, you only looked astray
Then I was told to leave, when I saw them take you away.

Don't you know that's hard for a little girl to take—that
you never cared though?
Through all the times of me crying an all the times I've caught you in
    lies
You said you were going to get better, in most of the many letters
I received over the years from you.

I guess it's time to let go of the rope I tried to get around you
I have realized that no amount of what I say about it
Will change you
You have to make that choice on your own
Daddy, I have to tell you something: you're not a child anymore
You, you're grown.

Bonnie Reimels
Milton, FL United States

Tenderness

Tentative eyes
Look at me perchance
Afraid of rejection
Dash hope in advance

Loves turned wrong
All but paralyzed
Shredded hearts wounded
Pain from betrayals and lies

Worn down and weary
Sick of running alone
We tell ourselves
Safer to have hearts of stone

You reach out to touch me
Feel my walls start to break
The warmth of your kiss
Seems to lessen the ache

And closer I feel
Your healing caress
Gently you soothe me
With your tenderness...

Melanie Hare
Leavenworth, KS United States

*I have been writing poems since I was a little girl! I have always considered poetry
a way to express my feelings and perceptions in a positive way.*

Habits

Chewed fingernails—jagged, tender
Scratching at the fight for originality
But stuck in old habits
Never remembering to floss
Taking off damp shoes in new homes
Shoplifting trifles and plastics for sport
Chiseling at the goodness of soul
For an undefined purpose
Namely the need to stay sane
While the truly reckless demons run amuck.

Never letting loose the servants of a storm
Never closing the bathroom doors
Chewing gum before bed
To keep my mouth from biting at my dreams.

The thing about fear is—
It tames the nightmares that encircle
But lets new ones fester and mold
The prevention becomes the creation.

Back-cracks when attracted to someone new
To keep my shoulders high
To watch for fighters, too.

Sam Parson
Commack, NY United States

Hey readers! I'm a high school junior living in New York, who has been avidly writing poetry for over five years. Writing is a source of sanctuary for me. I feel connected to my soul and my universe when I write. My spirit has been most influenced by my family, my love of the English language, and my continuing exploration of human emotion. I try to fully immerse myself in my passion for writing and expression. I also love literature, film and philosophy. I'm addicted to being ridiculous, and I don't think I'll ever stop biting my nails. Writing tames me, heals me, empowers me and sculpts me. I write to give voice to tempest; I write in the wrestle for humanity.

Friendship

Many people have many friends,
Some just have one or two.
These can be friends we have grown-up with,
or friends we have only known for a few years.
These friends will make big impacts on our life.

These friends will never leave us, nor will they forsake us.
These friends are there when things get tough;
They are there to offer us a hug or a shoulder to cry on,
They are there to offer advice on life or the struggles we are facing.
They never laugh at our failures—they are always there to cheer us on.
Friends we meet today may be the friendships that will last a lifetime…

Anna L. Morrison
Oxford, PA United States

Lock and Key

I set out
A walk to clear my head and cloud my mind.
Breathe deep and let your mind soar
And forget why you wanted to forget why.

And maybe just for *once* it'll all make sense.
And maybe just for once you'll get it right.
And *maybe,* just for *once,* someone else will understand.

Give me your hand.
I want to tell you
Everything.
I want you to know how much of me I would give
To you.
I want to tell you my dark past and
I want you to lock it away and
I want you and
I want you.

William Barber
Medina, NY United States

I'm currently a film student at the Rochester Institute of Technology in Rochester NY. I write what I feel, which is mostly rather dark. I love to have my work seen, even if I am unaware of who is reading it, because there is always that hope I will really connect with someone.

When Love Goes Away

When rainbows no longer come with a big pot of gold
When butterflies and moonbeams in our hands we can hold
When bright stars we wish upon seem to disappear
When songs of a love that's lost no longer brings a tear

When hearts full of love turn into stone
When two loves are parted and each left alone
When birds chirping sweetly can no longer be heard
When the vision of a loved one becomes cloudy and blurred

When the stings of a violin are broken forever
When the chances of true love become reduced to never
When life becomes much too painful to endure one more day
Then the soft sounds of an angel's wings I will hear, I pray
To gather me up, and take me away.

David Shadwell
Houston, TX United States

I began writing poetry in July 2008. I met a beautiful woman from Tasmania, who now lives in London. I discovered so quickly that we were true soul twins. We were together every day and evening for two weeks, constantly talking, laughing, crying, sharing secrets, and dancing. Before long, we could finish each other's sentences and knew we were destined to be best friends forever, with the added bonus of being soul twins. We are both in committed relationships with others, who fortunately have realized how extraordinary our relationship is. Jodi Sue Tanner lives in London and I live in Houston, but we have managed to be together on a number of trips, each one adding more inspiration for my poetry. I visited her in London this year, and we went to Westminster Abbey one day; I visited the gravesite of my ancestor, Thomas Shadwell, Poet Laureate to the Crown in the seventeenth century. More Inspiration! Jodi and her fiancé, Nick, are coming to spend Christmas with me this year and also bring in the new year in New Orleans. I have written a lot of poetry, which I hope to have published, and always have poetic thoughts going through my mind. I've always been a romantic and finally have the wisdom to write these thoughts and feelings down with pen on paper!

Nevermore

Feeling so lonely, feeling so blue
Trying so hard to get over you
Feeling the rejection, feeling the pain
Knowing in my heart things will never be the same
We tried so hard to make it work
But as fate has it, it was never meant to be
One day, I will be over you and the pain will go away
One day, I will accept that you will never be mine
Maybe one day I'll wake up and realize I'll be just fine
But for now, the pain is still there—the emptiness
the long lonely hours, the depression I must go through
After all the years of being hurt
lost and rejected, time and time again
I don't know if I will ever love again, or even want to
My heart, my mind, my soul was so full of love for you
I thought I had found happiness at last
But now that's gone, just an empty place remains
Null and void, just wiped away
Nevermore to be the same

Nancy Graham
Powell, TN United States

Heart Broke

While walking through the pieces of his broken heart,
She wondered what could cause it all to fall apart...

So down the Trail of Torment is where she would start,
To seek out the reason for this broken heart.

She came upon a puddle of pain she had to step around,
Filled with drops of blue that had been falling down.

Then she almost fell into a hole of hopelessness,
Deep with despair and lined with loneliness.

At the foot of Mount Rejection, his pride was found there—
Lost when he begged her back, and she left without a care.

She found his broken spirit, of this she was certain,
Scattered throughout the Desert of Desertion.

Then she came upon him weeping in distress,
His tears had filled the sea of Sadness.

She knelt beside him and asked what could make a man so blue,
And hung her head in shame when he answered...only you.

Jerry Vickrey
Del City, OK United States

You Are...My Mother

You are...
Someone I can count on,
I can call my friend.
Someone who will be there
forever, until the end.

You are...
Someone I can learn from
and teach a few things to.
Someone I can trust—
a friend who is true blue.

You are...
Someone I can run to
when I feel alone,
Someone who can make
any place feel like home.

You are...someone who has been there
from the very first breath.
Someone who has stuck by me
and never, ever left.

You are....my mother

Ian Milby
Aurora, CO United States

I am a junior at Smoky Hill High School in Aurora, CO. I am seventeen years old. My mother was the motivation behind writing "You Are...My Mother." I want to extend a special thank you to my mother, Christa, who has raised me by herself for the past fourteen years. Also, thanks to my friends at Smoky Hill High School. Be sure to look out for more poems by me in the future.

This Is My Wish

we all have wishes and dreams
and then there's fantasies and realities
if we don't like what we've become
there's so many things that we wish upon
it's okay to have these wishes
but make the dreams come true
you are the one that sets your path
but remember: reality is part of the math
I know who I want to be
but it's just the fantasy that sets me free
I suppose I can try and try
but would my life just be a lie?
I am who I am
because this is my life
this is the path that was set for me
in hope that one day my childhood fantasy
be my reality and not just a dream
this is my wish

Carlyne Segura
San Diego, CA United States

A Fond Farewell

Sweet words of comfort, love and affection
Flowing and expressing your emotion
Offering my soul so little protection
From any untrue uttering of devotion
And yes, I didn't rush to love you.

Tender embraces of warmth beyond compare
Caressing and fondling your hand in mine
Giving my heart so little care
From any sign not genuine
And yes, my fondness slowly grew.

Changeable moods, swinging to and fro
Hinting at jealously with some other
Suppressing my feelings to grow
From friendship to my forever lover
And yes, that is what you do.

Real love offers freedom and liberty
The heart finds its own way home
Let's not prolong this anguish and agony
Of breaking up and being on our own
And yes, fond farewell—adieu.

Helen Armstrong
Glasgow, Scotland United Kingdom

Indifference

Black as emptiness
  and forged in the furnace of uncertainty,
    this mighty stallion trots the streets of the living
      in search of compassion and mercy.

Upon his back sits a rider cloaked in the robe of a million starving faces.

He pulls back on the reigns of the unfeeling;
  as the stallion raises his head,
    sparks of detachment spewing from his nostrils.

Surrounding him are the spirits of the unemotional and heartless,
  causing him to shiver.

Raising his mighty hooves,
  he pounds the cobblestones made of disregard and detachment.

His flowing mane and tail, made of the poor and the suffering,
  ignites into a plea for generosity.

Greediness lines the pockets of many,
  but from the shadows comes one,
    draped in a long robe of charity.

Stepping forth, he casts his robe upon the rider and stallion—
  The seemingly impenetrable blackness lightens to gray.

P. R. Deremer
Salem, OR United States

To me, life is poetry. Every second of the day and night, new poems are created, whether spoken or merely seen. Poetry surrounds us: we breathe it in, just as we breathe in air. We witness it in a sunset or sunrise. It joins us when we're born, it survives us in death. Poetry can bring clarity to our emotions. It can bring us to new heights; it can cause us to experience new lows. Poetry is the instrument that brings music to our life symphony.

All American

My skin could be any color, it really doesn't matter
America is freedom served on a golden platter.
No hyphen, no split loyalty for me
My parents may not be American, or they just might be.

My spoken English might be perfect, or it may not be so
I could be by myself, or have a family with children in tow.
Being careful, as bringing what I left behind
Could jeopardize the very life I came to find.

Some in America have an "owe me" attitude,
Instead of having respect and gratitude.
Yes, gratitude for the original American
Who built America with freedom for all, in spite of fears.

America's original forefathers gathered together
Traveling through rough terrain and bad weather.
For freedom, they signed the Declaration of Independence
Against unfair taxes, they declared war in defiance.

We cannot be quiet when truth must be spoken,
Because this will cause America to be broken.
Unlike the rainbow, Truth is not just a token
Truth is the voice of insight that has awoken.

No hyphen description will I accept today
I will never have a half-loyalty debt to pay.
Gratitude for the freedom to be the best that I can
Appreciating the privilege to be All American.

Elaine Carroll Kelley
Riverside, CA United States

The writing bug hit me at an early age, but my parents felt it was a waste of my time. Writing in my teen years was done in secret. My senior year English teacher was the only person in those years to give me positive feedback for my writing. Upon retiring, I finally began creative writing classes. I am writing children's books and my memoirs. Writing poems has helped steady me through life's roller coaster. Often my poems desire to write themselves, and I just take notes. Thank you for the opportunity to have my poem published.

Hakuna Matata

Living peacefully while rested winds breeze through
trees whispering the great wonders of life
Worry-free as I walk on concrete stone that can
hypnotize the mind where one assumes the world
to be negative every waking moment

Existing in a perfect vision where money has no option
to rule or be ruled, eliminating stressful encounters that
evil beings present has never be easier in a state of clarity

A problem-free philosophy wielded by few but not
unteachable to many, opening gates and doors
to your utopia, Living peacefully while the sun
shines on success and the rain washes away depression
Viewing life in through the Hakuna Matata will make your
daily stroll through beautiful skies and dark clouds
worry less about antagonistic pleasures.

Courtney Bullock
Central Islip, NY United States

Courtney Shaun Poet is who I am; I can go on and on about what motivates me. Long story short, I'll say life keeps my pen trucking: memories, new experiences, love, hate, etc. I used to write love poems. At that time it was fairly easy with roses are red, but then I thought to explain why the rose was red. I see poetry as a lifestyle; it's something I do daily. Whatever comes to mind, if I can grasp its poetic taste, I'll take a sip and spill my beautiful words on the page. Poetry is me.

Freedom

As we all know, freedom isn't free
Look all around, and you can see
The brave men and women who have given their lives
Leaving loved ones alone—a child, a husband, a wife

What is war? To think it makes me sad
I just want the home; is that so bad?
Every day, we hear of another life taken
Where families are shattered and shaken

When will this end, all of the heartache?
When more soldiers die? Come on, for God's sake
Let this battle cease and send them home
Where they are safe and able to roam

We fly our flag so proudly, that's true
We love these colors: the red, white and blue
As we lose another casualty, you see
It's flown half-staff, and that's the way it be

They are not afraid, and they know how to fight
For what they know, for what is right
They are taught to be tough for you and me
When all the troops are home, then we'll stand up with glee

Anita Gould
Granite Falls, WA United States

I appreciate you letting me share my poetry. I love writing poetry. It seems to come easily to me—words just tend to flow. I live in Washington State and have been married for thirty-two years. I have four boys and one girl. I have fifteen grandchildren and a great-grandchild on the way. I work as at a hospital as a centralized scheduler: I schedule everything for the hospital, except surgeries. I hope this poem brings pleasure to the readers. Thank you for letting me share.

Vinimus-Vidimus-Vicimus

Brilliant golden rays of light
Illuminating the worn rock-strewn path
Baby blue jays chanting their hymn of hunger
Emerald green crickets playing their morning song
Dark, ominous clouds herald the approach of a
Wonderfully depressing, spirit-uplifting storm
A storm of whirling, chasing light vs. dark emotions
Anger, avarice, lust, envy, greed, love, sadness
All swirling and blending in a big hurricane of confusion
Ripping piece by piece
Mind, body, and soul
'Til there is naught but ghostly white twisted broken bones
Laying alone begging
Empty, lifeless, soulless, cobalt orbs gazing at the clear sapphire sky
Golden yellow sun and white fluffy marshmallow clouds
Salty air of ocean beaches drifts lazily on a gentle breeze
Fiery ruby red Robins singing harmoniously with blue jays
Soaring upward towards the light-giving smiling golden sun

Nathen Christian
Coram, NY United States

I am an eighteen-year-old college student, and I'm a member of the N.Y.S. National Guard. I have been writing poetry since the seventh grade and find it relaxing.

Spring Sacrifice

Inspired by the rite of spring

Earth speaks.
Her worldwide womb—
   through every bud's unfurling
     of her being—speaks.

I speak.
My own life's focus—
   opening my soul
     through earth's composing—speaks.

Earth sings.
Her woodland's choir—
   arousing all her life
     to birth her young joys—sings.

I sing.
My own delight—
   revitalizing earth's
     Wise vision—sings.

Earth dances.
Her bliss—
   the sun's direction lifts
     to choreograph his passion—dances.

I dance.
My own momentum
   moves my body's being and I dance—dance
     Lights dance, earth's joy, my life: my life
       for the earth—for earth's life—I dance.

Roy Sadler
Stourbridge, AL United Kingdom

I am an actor and poet living in Stourbridge in the English West Midlands. In the nineties I performed throughout Europe with Volcano Theatre in The Town That Went Mad a version of Dylan Thomas' Under Milk Wood and some other plays. I am preparing my spiritual and nature poetry, The Depths of Light, written over the last thirty years, for publication; and my translation of Rudolf Steiner's Calendar of the Soul, which I regard as the world's greatest mantric verse, will be published next year by Wynstones Press.

The End

My broken heart, it does not feel
It is numb
As I kneel
Silent, waiting
I used to think I could heal
But I'm still broken, hating
Hating how you left me
All alone as I crumbled
Becoming dust
I see
The metal of your cold heart as it starts to rust
Gentle, unbreathing I am
Still that broken feeling
In the dark
Kneeling
Bleeding
No feeling
And here it ends
Peace, silence
Chilled sadness

Guinevere Hatlelid
Abilene, KS United States

Poetry is my life, my way of relief. When I'm depressed, it's how I get back on my feet—how I express myself. It's glorious sadness and dread; it's happiness, joy, melody and rhythm. It's having the strength to move on, or even being stuck.

Eternal Bond

Her eyes glittered with tears as she laid the bundle down
A little face with pink ears, he never made a sound
She hovered over him and then slowly turned away
From where her most valuable possession lay
Finally, the baby started to cry, and it was heard loud and clear
By the lady of the house who took him in—her eyes full of fear
When the family saw him, they were outraged
For all they found was a note saying, "Keep him safe," followed by his age
Ten years later, the family moved to a villa two streets away
When they got there, the boy saw a garden and a dog running astray
A fortnight passed; and to his surprise, he found a letter in some loam
It told the story of the baby on the doorstep, an infant in need of a home
A river of tears streamed from his eyes as he read it over twice
He packed his trunk and stepped outside into the air that was cold as ice
"Are you my mother?" was all he asked, as he traveled through the town
At the end of the day, success befell, and he whirled around
There she was, encased by darkness—in a tattered, worn gown
There were laughter and tears as they hugged, and then his mother fell
    down
She was weak and frail and also poor, yet she had lived to see this day
Only to see her baby boy when she was taken away
This time, the tears came like a flood, and the boy was on his knees
When the tears were gone, he left the world…swept away by the breeze
He was taken to a magical place, where his mother had been waiting
He spotted her and gave her one more hug, his heart no longer aching
When they pulled away, all he had to say was
"Mommy, never leave me alone. Never go away."

Samyuktha Ravikumar
Irvine, CA United States

Samyuktha Ravikumar was born March 7, 1998 and is an emerging contemporary poet. She wrote her first poem when she was eight years old as a gift to her mom for Mother's day. Since then, she has been an avid poetry writer. Samyuktha's poems are usually very heartfelt—most of them describe emotional moments, such as the birth of a sibling or the loss of a treasured pet. These poems have touched the hearts of many people and have helped them open their eyes to the real world. Her first published poem is "Eternal Bond." Samyuktha takes great pride in her work and plans to broaden her horizons in the poetic field. When she is not writing poems, Samyuktha likes to read, sing, and golf.

Too Advanced

I take it day by day
Nothing I can do
I sit back and watch
As the world comes unglued

The world is falling apart
Nothing will get in its way
Electronics are killing us
Causing the world to decay

I'm just one person
It's not enough
People do what they wanna do
They don't five a f***

We need to go back
Go back in time
Many years ago
When people had their own minds

With all the advances
No one has to think
This is the problem
Why can't you people see?

Paula Mayabb
Quartz Hill, CA United States

The Human Touch

Love is the most powerful of all human emotions
It can heal, it can forgive and it can ignite the soul
The human touch is magic like no other
This is why I can call others my sister and my brother
Too often we forget that kindness doesn't cost anything
Know that the human touch is an energy
Awaiting to become a synergy in a time of joy or adversity
Recall the tragedy of 9/11
When the world stopped for a moment and became one
Many shared the pain and the loss
We sometimes forget what such an experience taught us
When we reach out to others and touch their lives
We are doing exactly what we were meant to do
The human touch is all about me and you
Think about times when someone gave you a smile
Remember the feeling as it only lasts for awhile
God never promised that life would be easy
But it is certainly worth living
The human touch reminds us how powerful we can be
Like a torch shining its light
And doing away with the darkness of the night
Let your human touch be felt and known
And others will know that they are not alone

Gerardo Angulo
Phoenix, AZ United States

Gerardo L. Angulo was born in Nogales, Sonora, Mexico. In 2002, I graduated from Northern Arizona University with a master's degree in counseling. I have worked in the human services profession for the past fourteen years. I currently work as a clinical supervisor helping to manage a program serving people living with HIV/AIDS. Currently, I am working on a master's degree in administration with Northern Arizona University. I have been fortunate and blessed to have had my poetry featured in various poetry anthology publications. I am a member and a board certified professional counselor with the American Psychotherapy Association.

My Daydreams Are My Life

My daydreams are my life
I perform on stage
The crowd goes wild
My voice reaches out
I sing into the night

My daydreams are my life
I go back in time
Fixing my mistakes
Changing my future

My daydreams are my life
I live during a disaster
Altering events just enough
To save life

I meet a man
Who seems so wrong
I make it right
We fall in love
My daydreams are my life

Sara Bloomberg
Boulder, CO United States

My Reflection

Lately when I look at my skin
I don't see scars, but stories I wrote
Others think they are scars
And for some time I did too
But I have to live with them
And each one has an untold story
Of how it came to be
How I wrote it, then regretted it
But now I realize
They help make me who I am
And enable me to live freely
Because my skin tells my story
Of how I got through four years of my life
And shows one of the struggles I've had
I'm not human if I don't have
Some hardships in my life
I can't hide them
So I might as well wear them the best I can
And if people don't like what they read
Then they can stop staring and get over it
Like I had to when I saw scars
And hated myself for doing it
Everyone has a story, but some people
Tell them in different ways
You can't judge a book by its cover
Just as you can't judge me by my skin

Andrea Nicole Hatter
Dowagiac, MI United States

Just Another Episode

What's going on in my head?
Oh no, it's the moment I dread
The voices are back
Please, go away
My world closes in and I can't focus
I sit for awhile hoping they will go away
So many voices but none are my own
This black emptiness is where I find myself
I just want to hide
I can't run, they will just follow me
I cry because I feel hopeless
Angry jumbled words fly at me from every direction
Silent tears fall, and I feel defeated
I close my eyes, and darkness surrounds me
Please, leave me alone!
Voices swirl around—never stopping, always talking
Minutes pass into hours.
I take a deep breath.
I scream until I can't anymore.
For a moment, I stop and I open my eyes.
Absolute silence.
They're gone...for now

Jennifer Figueroa
Long Branch, NJ United States

I'm a full-time college student who lives in New Jersey. I wrote this poem after I had the worst episode of my life. I had been dealing with schizoaffective disorder for a few years, but had not experienced numerous encounters with "voices" for a very long time. At first, I was scared and confused; but you learn to adjust to the weirdness of the situation. A very good friend of mine told me, "Insanity breeds genius." I hope someday people with mental illness will be heard. Until that day, I'll speak for them.

Evening Tableau

Evening spread her flaming colors across the west
Expertly painting the exquisite sunset hues
Deftly mixing them and doing her very best
To blend golden tones with grays and blues

Mixing shades of crimson gold and green
Spreading saffron ribbons upon the heavens wide
Trimming the sky with lovely lavender streams
Wherein the evening star will ride

The sunset is now gloriously complete
Having had its one short wondrous hour
Before night could steal from her retreat
And call her minions from their bower

Glory Posey
Dallas, TX United States

Decision-Making

You pull me
This way and that
I can't stand this
You're always stringing me along
Make a decision
Me or her
You have to choose but
I know you can't
So I'll choose
It's over
I'm done
No need for crying
I know you were with me just for fun

Destiny Cooper
Houston, TX United States

Stevie

An idol in the making
at just fifteen
words on paper
she started to sing.

Unique by herself
but great in a band
her voice was the reason
she had millions of fans.

Smoking cigarettes
for marriage and loss
but she had to quit
for her voice was the cost.

But still the world loved her
from her outfits to her name
and for those reasons
she rose to fame.

Born Stephanie Lynn
on May twenty-sixth
but known by the words
as the great Stevie Nicks.

Leah Murfin
Quincy, IL United States

No Giving Up

When everything is lost and you stand in a barren land,
you might sway under such an emotional distress and hatred.
By the rushing feelings of desperation and sadness,
you crouched down and cried out the hot tears.

When you failed everything and had no friends to depend on,
you looked around—desperate to find the shelter from the evil.
By the loneliness, by the feeling of betrayal,
you looked up and bellowed like a mad man.

In the barren land, in the evil place,
you have walked too far, and yet not far from turning back.
In the feelings of hatred, feelings of sadness,
you have felt too many evil things and yet not far from feeling the
    opposite.

There might be a vast barren land, and there might be an evil place—
But if you walk through every day, every night,
if you count on your every step, not stumbling, but proudly,
there might be an open way for you.

No matter how much you've suffered, no matter how much you've in
    vain,
just know that it is not the end.
Until you walk the long journey that you cannot turn back,
until you wither to nothing, and until you feel no more of our world,
there is no giving up.

Seungil Lee
San Marino, CA United States

It Feels Right

The waves of turmoil are never mine
With the blessings coming in His due time
Controversy shadows our every day
As we bargain and barter everyone's dismay
Propagate the years and what do you see?
A merciful angel with wings for me
This glimmer of hope which has faith at its base
Will shine forth with beauty at His glorious face
Today is gone and tomorrow feels right
To underscore a journey with humility and fight
No more anxiety of what will be
Soaring with wings, just you and me
The time is now, the time is right
So let go of shadows hindering the night
I love this life, by grace I'm here
Never forgetting the drop of my lonely tear
Complications are mystical in the world of deceit
Only to be hampered by my standing two feet
I will never rule by a prideful display
As we are here to worship and daily pray
My protector and guide will never let me down
Because once I was lost, and now I'm found

Bill Case
Houston, TX United States

*I have written numerous poems reflecting on my personal journey throughout the
years. Each is inspired and heartfelt when put in words.*

Wandering Night

Still is the night that wanders
Through thick and merciless fire,
Yet fails to sound the siren call
As dawn, it must acquire.
Across a gentle breeze is heard
The crackle of a flame;
As smoke devours, undeterred—
Inferno taking claim.
Through thick and thin, though blistered now,
Darkness leaves a trail
And rids itself of heavy weight;
The light will soon prevail.

Fluid is the day that dribbles,
That drowns in sky and grass—
Seeping into all that thrives
Off fulgor, and en masse.
A radiant ball of burning gas,
So bright and luminous,
Draws out life from near and far
In pools, bituminous,
And sets a dwindling world ablaze;
Prepares it for a fight
With smoke that hovers, floats and curls
Into a wandering night.

Shannon Armstrong
Kingston, ON Canada

Inner Man

There is an inner man
That grows and grows.
No one knows
Which way it will go.
It is like branches of a tree
Growing this way and that.
Who can say
Who can say
Today, where it is at?
Some branches are fine.
Some branches are strong.
Some branches have beauty.
Some branches have thorns.
The tree being a beauty
A haven for some.
That same tree being,
Nourishment for others,
To replenish the kingdom.
Those thorns—
They hurt, they pierce
They cause bleeding, too.
You can obtain
All this wisdom
From that inner man: you.

Susanna Hart
Rochester, MI United States

Untitled

It was hard to watch death's cold hands
Pry you from life's warm ones—
Suffering in undeserved pain,
Everyone thinking you would be okay.
No one was ready to face the end.
A dry eye was not found;
your sparkling ones weren't either.
Laughter echoed from reminiscent stories,
but your laughter was not heard
on the afternoon of your funeral.
Holidays will never be the same,
though your presence will still surround.
No one wanted your life to end—
Loved always, as Uncle Stephen.

Melissa Cospito
Ormond Beach, FL United States

Warmth

We sit and talk for the first time alone
Thoughts are deep as are questioning eyes
Who are we, and why do we feel like this?
With her hand in mine, we exhibit no denies
The warmth I feel inspires perplexity, because
The delight it brings should not be mine
But the pain it provokes is pleasure in disguise
Heating the intent of my desirous design
As we speak, our eyes affix in place
To see beyond ourselves, we cannot
Warmth beams with every selfish glance
And brings us closer to, who knows what?
The voice I listen to is filled with warmth
Every word draws me as a moth to the flame
What she says captures me like a covert snare
And embraces me, which is her deliberate aim
Our hearts combine to envelop our needs
Their resounding beats create warmth within
Our souls fuse with the strength of steel
Forging a love that can never part again
Lavish love is the treasure in our eyes
But only its fictional worth is ours to discover
Yet, that fiery flame lives since we sat and talked
So each will never lose the warmth of a lover

Dick Cullen
Apopka, FL United States

This poem is a bit philosophical, yet speaks to an episode in my life, which has a deep fibrous interconnecting hold established between a certain someone and myself that is so very precious in my heart. I am a retired carpenter who has always been dabbling in the writing of lyrics, but hasn't really been seriously attached to such an endeavor. It was not until a few years ago that I found I had time on my hands and the need to write about profound changes in life...and an inspiring love standing near.

I Cry

I cry not only for what you're leaving behind,
But for who you were when you were still around.

It may seem that I am looking at the present,
As if to say you have already passed,
But it is only in preparation for the future.

I see you now and I look back—
Back at the days
When we could walk and talk together.
But now it seems time is slipping away, faster than I can run.

I dread the day you leave me here,
Stranded…facing the world alone.

I wish God could understand how I feel:
Your time is not now, not this way.

If anything, let Him take me instead.

I need you now—more than I ever have—
and, I guess this means your job is done.

So I must tell you:
I cry not only for what you're leaving behind,
But for who you were when you were still around.

Ashlea Maddex
North York, ON Canada

I am nineteen years old and a professional track and field athlete. I write to express my feelings. This particular poem was written the day before my beloved grandfather passed away on August 7, 2007.

Little Miracle

Little Miracle, sleeping in my arms,
Little Miracle, I'll try to keep you from harm.
You've changed my life in so many ways,
and you've only lived for just a few days.
Little Miracle, so pretty and small,
will you be short or will you be tall?
Time will tell and we'll wait and see
and watch what you will grow up to be.
So blessed is my life now that you are here—
God has given me a gift so dear.
Little Miracle, you bring all such joy and happiness.
Your facial expressions are the best!
Little Miracle, you'll grow up too fast;
but I'll hold on to these memories and take pictures that last.
Little Miracle, my sweet baby girl,
You are my everything, my whole world.
Little Miracle, your mother am I—
and my love for you reaches up past the sky.
I love you now and I'll love you then,
with a love that lasts and will never end.

Lachelle Speaker
Victoria, TX United States

I am a school teacher, small business owner, poet, wife and new mother. This poem is inspired by my precious baby girl, for whom we waited years and years. She is a true miracle, and we are greatly blessed to have her. She has forever changed our lives, and even though she has only been here a very short time, life will never be the same; life has more meaning, and I am the happiest I've ever been. I love my Little Miracle.

Angel

You shine like a star
as bright as can be
with wings as light
as a feather.

Your halo is bright,
lovely as ever
a silk dress on your body
lightly colored, of course.

As I take your hand
and you lead me away,
I smile and say:
"So, this is a piece of Heaven."

Amanda Powers
Cresco, IA United States

A Moment in Time

The world stops spinning for a moment in time.
When you walk in the room, your eyes lock on mine.

Your icy-blue eyes and light brown hair,
How can I help not to stop and stare?

You're not the cutest or the best in shape.
There's just something about you I can't escape.

When you smile, I melt where I stand.
Oh, how I'd love to be holding your hand.

You walk away slowly, as if wanting to speak—
We both remain silent, not making a peep.

I know God has a man somewhere waiting for me,
I often wonder when that will be.

Icy blue eyes stare back at mine,
The world stops spinning for a moment in time.

Kandi Ritton
Horseheads, NY United States

I currently work as a keyboard specialist in New York State department of corrections. I have written most of my life—mostly short stories—but have recently discovered poetry and have thoroughly enjoyed it. It's nice to be able to write your frustrations into a poem, or make up a complete story in just a few lines. Besides writing, I enjoy spending time with my family and pets (we own five cats and six dogs), camping, roller blading, and walking.

Future Is Now

When I grow old,
You'll be by my side—
You'll try to keep me standing,
All throughout my life.

When I grow old,
You'll cry with and for me.
I have become so cold,
Lost in the seven seas.

I have grown so old,
My soul is withering;
Please travel on,
With or without me.

Carin Belen Adame
Tacoma, WA United States

Fears

We were once lovers—another time, another place.
I felt it the moment I first saw your face.
I pushed the thought, the feelings aside;
Many nights, my thoughts of you I would hide.

For years I wanted you, I was held back by fear—
You awakened something in me whenever you were near.
It was as if there was something my heart knew,
For I was only happy when I got to see you.

Every time you came walking through that door,
You left with me wanting to talk with you more.
If I had only trusted what my heart was trying to say...
I never wanted you to leave, I wanted you to stay.

I almost lost you again because of my fears;
When I think about that, out flow the tears.
But you were persistent, as if your heart knew too,
It was always meant to be—me and you.

Mary Legue
Vassar, MI United States

I began writing poetry occasionally in high school, but have lost all that I wrote back then with the exception of the poems I wrote for my stillborn daughter twenty-eight years ago. I started writing again because of one man—my best friend and the love of my life. He inspires me like no one else ever could, and I thank God every day for bringing us together. Thank you, Wayne, for loving me, inspiring me and encouraging me. I love you very much.

Uncluttered

Wildflowers go on forever
passing in time—
A crossing of distant memories
from earth to sky.
She lay dreaming
beyond the purple haze
to a simple life
uncluttered.

Chevelle Wernsmann
Brush, CO United States

I am an adult survivor of child sexual abuse. From the depths of our darkest hours to the very nature of our survival, we stand constantly growing, living, changing: surviving. For all who have helped that one child survive, we thank you.

Moving On

One tree stands divided
uprooted from the earth
sap flowing from severed limbs,
empty holes about its girth.

The shaded half begs for sun
the exposed half begs for rain;
one tree stands divided
when once it was the same.

Seasons pass this fruitless mass
as time begins to mend.
Leaves are shed, yellow-brown from red
oh, time is but a friend!

Now two trees stand on two plots of land
both with equal view.
Willows weep and fichus creep
courageous are the few.

Carol Orourke
Santa Monica, CA United States

I have the gift of observation. I feel the joy, laughter, tears and pain of others. I have published books, screenplays and poems.

Cocoon

I am in a cocoon
I am safe,
And I am warm.
As I lie curled up
In my cocoon,
As war is fought.
I feel for my wings
But they aren't there yet
So I cannot spread my wings
To fly away and fight the fight
They told me that being a butterfly would be easy
But it is not.
To be pretty you must be ugly,
To be ugly you must be scary.
To be scary you must be mean.
That is not me;
My cause is not mean.
I cannot be a butterfly like my peers.
I'll just stay
In my nice cocoon
My silky-sweet
Warm and loving
Cocoon

Melanie Weeks
Ball, LA United States

My poems are a reflection of me, and some have underlying meanings. I have my faith, but I also have depression and anger. I love my family and friends. I have been deceived, and I have been the deceiver. I try to put feeling in what I write, and I hope that the reader will feel it.

Untitled

Sleepless nights
begin to take
their toll
all the repressed
feelings come
to the surface
weak and
vulnerable to
the barrage
of emotions I'm
not ready to
face.

Amanda Jo Humphreys
Glendale, AZ United States

What to Write, September 10, 2012

What to write, what to write…
There are so many things on my mind!
I could write about that one guy I like.
You know,
That blond haired boy in my geometry class...
No.
Oh! Maybe that the leaves are changing,
About how pretty they're getting.
Nah.
What about that new cheer gym I joined?
Or maybe…
Never mind, I already wrote about that.
I think I have an idea,
I just hope it works.
Okay,
Here I go…
What to write, what to write…

Tiffany McBain
Saint Charles, MO United States

Path

I'm on my way—where I'm going, I'm not sure
I'm just letting my feet take me
I'm not in a hurry, and I'm not taking my time
I'm at just the right pace to get me where I have to
Enjoying everything on my way
Stopping when I want to or have to
But I always keep going
Taking the paths I chose
Learning me
Creating me
Forming me into who I am and always will be
Ever changing the way I see things and act upon things that block my
path
Things hindering me from staying on the same path
Forcing me to choose another
Although my destination stayed the same
All the things on my way changed
Making me into something different
The old path led me to this one
So this one will lead me to another

Anthony King
Fort Plain, NY United States

Passion

The night was so passionate
Your sweet love took me into your arms, my dear
Your loving touch and tender kisses are so compassionate
I felt the wind washing away my tear
My body moves to each kiss it releases
Was this really happening to me?
I wasn't imaging as the passion inside me increases
I was free, free into the gates of eternal love
My angel stared into my eyes on this still earth
Happiness came over me as you fell over my shoulders
You blew in me the breath of life as I gave birth
I knew I could always be with you; there were no others
Forever and ever, every moment we share
You show your devotion forever more
I never doubted you because of how much you care
I am glad now because I know for sure
Mi Amore, as they would say in Spanish
Your love has taken over me and my soul into resurrection
I love it with my neglected heart, but I can stand this
I have given you my all and that's the right direction
I don't want to lose or abuse you, because you are my love passion

Dalston Harrison
Brooklyn, NY United States

I am truly a hard-working man in this world, and I treasure my family and my loved ones. I love writing poetry; I have been writing all my life. I was born and raised in Brooklyn. I love all of my children equally and most importantly, I love both my parents who brought me into this world.

The Time Is Now

I pledge

You can't break me this time, for this time I'll be careful
You can't take away my glory anymore

I'll overcome all the wreckage that is paving my way, and this time I
won't fall
I'll get over all the debris; I'll get through it all

So this time, I won't break

I can't break...

I've got to stay strong and this is for my own sake

I question if the position I'm in is where I belong
It feels like a provisional place that I've been in for much too long

I've got to fight the certainty, or maybe even a comforting prospect
There no longer lies a reason for sugar-coating or emotional neglect
No more cynicism, and no more regrets

I will stay whole this time around, because I pledge not to break
I must stay complete, for my heart's sake

Lovely Chantal Maxwell
San Pedro, CA United States

*I've always been fascinated with poetry and literature. I idolize poets like Emily
Dickinson, Marina Tsvetaeva and Fransesca Lia Block. Poetry is my passion.*

Love Like Rain

Thoughts of her cloud my vision like the sky on a rainy day.
The gentle breeze tugs and pushes me along,
Through my daydreams of her.
Soft droplets of water leaving their lasting mark on my cheek,
Reminiscent of her kiss.
Rain water pools on the ground, creating temporary mirrors
Of her reflection for me.
The wind picks up, and I cannot see.
I can't tell if it's the rain or my tears
Blinding me in her absence.
A warm embrace washes over me, like holding her in my arms.
I know it means she is thinking the same about me,
In her own rain so far away.

Catlin Marchand
Las Vegas, NV United States

I am twenty-seven years old and a resident of Las Vegas, NV. Writing has always been a quiet and therapeutic hobby. Along with poetry, I have interests in theatre, and I attended the Las Vegas Academy of Preforming Arts. I have few close friends, but those closest to me are heavy influences in my writing.

They Sit

The days are so long, and the nights, they are too;
They sit and they wait, with very little to do.
The days when they were young and fit
Have long been gone, and now they sit.
Remembering their youth, the fun that they had,
And now they spend so many hours in bed.

They wait for a visit from a daughter or son,
Whose day will be busy until it is done.
But a smile and a hug are so often what's needed;
And sometimes, this longing just goes by unheeded.

So, as you go through the average day in your life
That is filled up with stress and rushing is rife,
Try to imagine no deadlines or hassles, the rest—
And think how you'd do, if put to the test!
So somehow make time for your mom or your dad,
And give them some time, the time that you had...
When they were rushed, stressed and working hard too,
To give the best in life that they could offer to you.

You will feel better, and they'll feel so good—
That with all of life's burdens, you understood
That all that they wanted was a hug and a kiss,
And this opportunity you would not miss.

Lorraine McLennan
Niagara Falls, ON Canada

This is another opportunity for me to express my feelings. Poetry has always interested me. I began writing a birthday poem for my dad when I was about fifteen or sixteen and have written on occasion for family and friends on birthdays, anniversaries and for other events ever since. I have now graduated to having written a book which is published. However, poetry is still of great interest to me. Nearing the age of eighty has given me a different perspective on life, one which is very satisfying. This poem, I am sure, expresses the feeling of many my age.

Peace

Above the waves, I wish I could be
Gently floating in an all-encompassing sea
Where hurt and pain are no more
Upon the angelic seashore
With love and grace brushing my being
Hearts with warmth forever empower me
Darkness washed away by light
Death reborn without the night
For the only one true and just
Is God the Father in whom we trust

Kathrine Vatcher
Kitchener, ON Canada

My first encounter with pen and paper was at a young age. I participated in public speaking and drama. I was introduced to the more eloquent writing of William Shakespeare's Romeo *and* Juliet *shortly thereafter. Intrigued with beautiful words, stories and poetry began to flow. I live with my husband, two daughters, two grandsons and a cat and dog in Kitchener, ON, Canada.*

Judging

Judging somebody is so easy to do
It's like breathing, because we don't even think about what we are doing
But we do not know everyone's life
Some people come from abusive families
Others have to care for their parents
Because the parents are too drunk or high
Then there are homeless who only get one meal a day
We do not take the time to realize how
Hurtful our words can be
We don't stop and put ourselves in another person's shoes
We just judge people based on their looks
Then we assign them to a group
Next time you want to judge someone
stop and think how hurtful your words might be
Do not judge, unless you want to be judged right back

Krystal Hanson
Lansing, IA United States

The Last Fall

Look at her face
So perfect, yet frail.

Even with the lace tied from her head to her tail
Still so perfect, even after that last taste of ale.

She made her mistakes subtotal in her mind as if it was just pretend
somehow knowing the day would come to a terrible end.

As that last tear fell from her eye
She now knew it was time.

Even in this lonesome rhyme,
She lent her ear for the worst of her fears.

She knew she could never fall
At least she knew, she was not eight feet tall.

Victoria Gipson
Marissa, IL United States

Grateful

Do thou not see the gift they create?
With gentle kiss comes love from hate.
For in thy arms one gently weeping
'Tis mine to care for 'til gently sleeping.
To share a dream 'til it comes true
Tis dreamed by one, but shared by two.
For if in Cupid's spell I am cast,
Be forever grateful for each day it doth last.

Natalia Small
Baulkham Hills, NSW Australia

Disordered Life

Sticks and stones will break my bones,
and all the words destroy me.
The mirror tells me who I am
and reflects back my story.
Trapped in a world of black and white,
the color keeps fading away.
I fell off the path so long ago,
when I starved myself that day.
Perfection is what it's all about,
I thought I had control.
But as it progressed,
I began to see
you had taken the throne.
Mirrors can lie,
but it's you that did the work.
I fell into your life;
then I was drowning in your hurt.
You consumed my entire life,
put me to the test—
fed me all those lies,
but deprived me of the rest.

Alyssa Kissel
Suffern, NY United States

At fourteen years old, some may think my main focuses are boys, friends, and hobbies. Although all are frequent thoughts, my main focus as of now is recovery from my eating disorder. It continues to be a journey, and through poetry and lyrics, I express my deepest thoughts and feelings. Poetry is an amazing outlet and an important part of my recovery.

Diamond Mind 2012

Set your mind as a diamond in the sky
Spread your wings and start to fly
It's time to let go of all that you know
Because you're invited to the greatest show

You see, I believe that you can create
Material form from a spiritual state
So you must practice and practice well
There's really no need to buy and sell!

All that glitters doesn't have to be gold
Sometimes it's a wonderful vision to behold
You know there is really nothing to lose
When at last you see the colour you choose

So take a step toward me
If in your mind's eye you want to see
Now is the time to materialize your dreams
Nothing in reality is what it seems

I've heard it said we all must awake
I know miracles don't happen just for my sake!
But even if it really did fall to me
I'm more than happy to enlighten humanity!

So will you try to set your mind
As the clearest of diamonds in the sky?
Your brain is capable of so much more
And 2012 is the first year we can explore.

Lucy Caxton Brown
Brighton, East Sussex United Kingdom

*This year, I published three poetry books: The Small Book of Poems, including
"Golden Ray" and "Cupid's Child"; an epic poem, called the* River Centaur; *and*
Castle in the Sky and Other Selected Poems. *One more epic poem is about
to be published. It is called "The Key." I am currently working on my fifth book
of poems, which I hope to have published soon. My hobbies include painting,
organic gardening and archaeology. My interests lay in sustainable development,
global politics, religion and archaeology. I hope my poetry inspires and brings
happiness to those who read it. I enjoy receiving feedback from readers and
blog occasionally.*

A Place That Time Has Forgotten

The mountains stand tall and strong
Reaching for the clouds and heavens above
And also for the sun that shines like glove, that stretches forth it's
finger's with love
Below them is a peaceful land
Filled with trees, rocks, birds and bees
Rivers flowing to reach the seas
A place that time has almost forgotten
A place of beauty in a world that has turned rotten
Sin abounds everywhere
People have stopped loving; no one any longer cares
It is time for the bow
Bow to your Lord and to the Master
Time; is drawing nearer, much faster
The end of the day
The end of the year
The Lord is calling
Do you hear?

Sharon King
Copperas Cove, TX United States

Things I've Learned About Math

Learning to do things
you already know—

Like adding, subtracting,
dividing and more.

Problems (no sense) thinking (no sense)
Can't figure out.

It's all the same,
Whether it's hard or easy.

Math…mystery…
adventure…all the same.

Compared to waiting,
it's so easy.

Multiplication, the hardest;
it hurts, just wait…
it'll strain your brain.

Learn math… I know,
It's boring. Oh yes,
Too bad…learn it.

Laura Hoeppner
Aurora, CO United States

Tender Moments

I treasure every breath we share
as our lips gently meet.
The flutter to my very soul
from kisses, oh so sweet.

The way your hands caress my face
sends shivers down my spine.
Your seeking eyes, they stole my heart,
until the end of time.

Loving words, a whispered thought,
they help my spirit mend.
The pleasures that you give to me,
they never seem to end.

Every moment spent with you
is priceless and sublime.
I'm proud and blessed to tell you now,
thank God that you are mine.

Angel Branikurt
Ragley, LA United States

I believe in the power of words—whether to inform, or as an instrument of release. We are all capable of great things, if we choose to follow the path on which our soul sends us. My path has been poetry. I hope the visions my poems inspire give a sense of unity to those who read them. I thank my family and friends for their love and support. Also, thank you to Dean Ahrens, who helped renew my sense of purpose.

When I Grow Old

When I grow old, I want you there
I want to know that you still care;
Regardless of weight or color hair
I want to know that we're still a pair.

Despite my wrinkles that may cause you fright,
Despite my body that won't work just right,
Despite my clothes that may fit too tight,
Open your arms, hold me, make it alright.

Look into my eyes, say you still love me;
The kids are all grown, so now it's just we.
We've branched away from our family tree—
Life's book is closing, just as it should be.

Alicia Land
Atlanta, GA United States

Childhood Days

Thinking back upon childhood days
How fun was found in so many ways.
Feeding hungry ducks in the park—
Playing hide and seek in the dark.
With my friends, sharing jokes to tell,
Wishing hard by the wishing-well.
Carnivals filled with magic arrive
Imaginations came alive.
Riding on the merry-go-round,
On my big horse—high off the ground.
Watching parades come to my town—
Big smiles made, never a frown.
My own memories help me to see
The joy of being young and free.
Such times stay with me from the past
Kept in my heart where they will last.

Julie Pisacane
Baldwin, NY United States

I am a published author of poetry books and children's Sunday school lessons at World Sunday School.com. I remain part of several online Christian writing ministries and thank the Lord for simply everything—my life, my family and all that our Lord of life has created.

Waves

For anything we have in life,
For everything we love,
It takes a lot to show your heart
And open yourself up.
To subject yourself to pain and tears,
To make your hopes and wishes known,
For who or what you care about
The hardest things to do:
Realizing you aren't alone anymore,
Accepting mistakes for what they are,
And seeing them float by us all
Like a slowly-sinking ship or boat.
Smiling at the darkest times,
And holding on, not letting go.
Fighting and trying and crying to not let it end;
Rebuilding enforcing and effort-strengthening the bonds.
Wind pushing us in all directions,
Slowing all the progress down—
Confusing and disorienting,
Dragging us down from our holds.
But if we suffer through it all,
If we can make it till the end…
What waits for us is worth the struggle.
For who can wait?
A loving, lifelong friend.

Sarah Garcia
Laramie, WY United States

One Perfect Rose

In my youth my garden grew
Nurtured through my love
Each blossom seemed so perfect,
warmed by the sun above.

Yet youth lasts not forever
With age my gardens grown
The most beautiful of roses-
Through seeds which love has sown.

The sun brought out their beauty
The moon brought the dew€"
Yet the loveliest of roses
Came from the love I have for you.

Time brings upon some changes
Petals have begun to fall-
One by one I've lost some beauty
Yet it matters not at all.

A rose garden lasts not forever
As summer fades away
No time to feed my garden
For daylight fails today,

I can no longer see my garden
Nor smell the fragrance of the rose-
But in my mind I clearly see
One perfect rose.

Sandra Hamilton
Jefferson, OR United States

Enough Is Enough

Enough is what I say
To all the lies, tears, and hate.
Enough with all the pain
Because I have nothing else to gain.

Why did everything have to change?
I swear I'm not insane,
I just want to be alone;
I just want to go back home.

This feeling is eating me alive,
I might have to say goodbye.
I try to be strong and fight,
But I can already feel their lights.

I want to cover my face and hide,
But now I have finally found some pride.
I won't be scared for what awaits—
I won't let my fear decide my fate.

Melissa Verdugo
Tucson, AZ United States

Lord, Father

Give us a day of breath, a day to breathe
As morning comes, Father above, giving
Us a day, awake, breathe
So many had fallen
Unfortunately into the streets
Is this the way it should be?
We throw it all away. Yesterday's dreams
Dawn so near; so many futures so unclear
As time comes, like a thief in the night
In many sights, is this right?
As Father above gives us
Time to make things right
We let a day fall into night
How could things be right?
Dark nights fall without lights or a call
We thrown it all away
Love had gone; time was lost and spent together no more
Given to awaken and breathe freely
Life is a candle on a hill
As winds begin to blow out the light,
Dawn so clear, no one could not hear the bells ring loud and clear
Fear sand of time's slipping away
Story of life—some had faded
Away, and lost the way home
It's better to pray than let a day get away

Mark Williams
Pomona, CA United States

*Poetry came unto me by pain and grace from my Father above. Without His love,
it would not be done. Only through stress I came to be blessed. In His mighty eyes,
I was able to write and shine. His words of love were put into my mind to reach
out in faith, to find the way into light. Now I see inside of me. From July 2011
through today, I have written poetry. I still pray and still struggle within my
spirit within me, but I lift up the gift of poetry that was dealt to me.*

Patterns

I thought of you today,
as I watched the wayward
patterns in the sky,
as I watched my failed
existence pass me by.
Similes of days gone by.
I thought of me,
and of the failures
I've been able to endure,
and of the hardships
that in life can be so sure.
Similes of life's duress.
I thought of us,
of all the times we had to say
one more goodbye,
of all the times
we had to sigh and wonder why.
I thought of times
when I could only sit and cry,
when life's misfortunes
make you wish a last goodbye.
Similes of life gone by.

Felipe Chacon Jr.
El Paso, TX United States

I am a sixty-one-year-old divorced male with three grown children—Randy, April and Rodney—and several grandkids. I am employed by the city of El Paso's transportation department as a traffic signs technician. I studied two years of college at UT-El Paso, where I majored in electrical engineering, English and creative writing. I call my poetry "The voice from within," because I've heard and felt this voice since I was very small.

The Seasons

Spring is like a blue-eyed maiden
Golden hair with flowers laden
That tiptoes softly on the breeze
Wishing all the world to please

Summer, a season of golden dreams
Raining dew upon green leaves
The sun, he reigns in all his glory
With all the stars around him soaring

Fall, a time of wind and bluster
With all the strength that it can muster
Calming into sunny days
Indian summer in all its ways

Winter, of which Jack Frost is king
Christmas pudding and other things
Snowmen, and snowballs flying high
But never quite touching the sky

Spring, summer, fall and winter
These are the seasons four
And I must say this is the end
You see, there are no more

Elisabeth Eye
Coolville, OH United States

Amy

They left Amy,
They left her tasting her own blood and swallowing her own teeth.
Beaten and left behind on a common street corner,
The men who took Amy's innocence hope she is dead.

These heartless men will be Amy's reason why she won't get close to
    any man,
Why none of her relationships will ever work out.
She will always blame these men for taking her innocence;
It'll be a while before she can even overcome this.
Amy's dead, she dies.

Her appearance is that of an old, broken pin-up doll;
Waves of tears ran through her pretty face and mixed with her white
    mascara.
Her pink cocktail dress riddled with blood and dirt—
Amy's underwear was drenched in both.

Locks of her black hair were ripped out,
Multiple stab wounds told the story of her struggle.
Though the story's end is unsightly,
As the light is missing from her hazel eyes...
Amy's alive, she lived.

Ozirus Morency
Union, NJ United States

My Neighbor Down the Hall

For years and years we've fought and fought
I'm right, you're wrong
That's mine, go away

We've screamed and yelled
And slammed countless doors
Then spent hours without speaking

As time goes by we do grow closer
And I worry more about you every day
You're smart and strong and talented beyond
But I still worry
That's how I show I care

I annoy you to no end
Mostly just because I know I can
You have your ways of getting even
Past, present, and in all the years to come this is how things are and
    will be

We take, we give
We laugh, we fight
Back and forth the comments go
And this is our happy normal

Despite it all, you're there for me
Same as I am for you
Always only a door away
So just take three steps down the hall, my little brother
And I'll be there—no matter what

Izzy Allen
Danville, NH United States

Sit and Wait

When I was a small child
I surely hated to sit and wait
In a doctor's office and imagine
What was going to be my fate

I pictured this long needle
At least a yardstick long
And I knew my parents had told him
About all the things that I had done wrong

Doc peered at me through his glasses
And asked, "How do you feel today?"
But I knew deep down in my heart
"I'm going to get you," is what he meant to say

He sure looked big when I was four
And said I needed my tonsils out
He'd stick that stick down my throat
And I'd wiggle all about

And Mom would say, "Behave yourself"
When I asked about the huge necklace around his neck
He put it on my chest and listened
Mom seemed to be a nervous wreck

A guy couldn't even have fun
When he went to see old Doc
Ya had to try and act proper
And that's hard to do for a little tot

Madelin V. Flannery
Peoria, AZ United States

Madelin Vaugn Waterman Flannery was born in Delhi, NY and learned from a small child to use poetry as a learning tool. If she put something in poetic form, it was easy to remember. She used poetry to teach some of life's lessons to her husband, John, and five children: April, Dixie, Bart, John Curtis, and Christina. She wore many hats and used her experiences in her poetry to often boost moods. Her family, whom she loves and adores, always came first. She loved making people happy and gave gifts of poems to them about them, to see them smile.

Sage and Time

From moment of memory, revisit of thought—
the puzzle, perplexing, but stop it will not.
With softened surroundings in loving pastels
she discovered too early that gentleness fails.

Clarity and purpose, she hungered for more,
her life understated yet richly bestowed.
To delight in the feeling, connections of love,
oh wondrous creations—must be from above.

Is that how is was on the day I began,
soon torn from your bliss, thrust forward by hand?
Holding my ears from the shock of a wail;
the coldness is something from which I won't heal.

Long on my journey to answer the call,
my colors now faded. Will they soften my fall?
Who comforts my senses and heightens my grace
to the levels I crave, for the anguish I face?

I use all that matters, my pinks and my grays,
and study the rhythms that beat out my days.
When I face life's decline and examine my page,
I will choose from all colors. Yet, where is my sage?

Victoria Grove
Woodbury, MN United States

I am from Woodbury, MN and live with my husband, Will. My interest in poetry began about ten years ago, while sitting in my kitchen. I have published several poems, covering many topics of interest to me. Although some have been personal, this poem is about an individual attempting to understand her life through the passage of time. I would like to dedicate "Sage and Time" to my sister, Laura Bergmeier Flattery, who lost her life this year. She was a wonderful influence with significant poetry-writing abilities of her own.

Listen

Listen, just listen, to the sway of the stream;
As it glistens quite softly, it feels like a dream.
Listen just listen, to the song of the bird—
The sweetest, calming sound ever heard.

Listen, just listen, to the innocent trees,
As the wind blows gently by their multicolored leaves.
Listen just listen, to the animals play,
Having secret conversations in their own magical way.

Listen, just listen, you are now in a different place—
A place with cities, cars, streets, and the human race.
Now listen, just listen to the loud crazy street:
People shouting, machines building, this is anything but neat.

Listen, just listen, to the fear of living things;
Habitats disappearing, this is what technology brings.
Listen, just listen, to the trees, quiet and afraid,
As workers begin their tree chopping raid.

Listen just listen, to the poor, frightened bird
Having no choice but to fly onward.
Listen, just listen, to the ill-treated stream;
Polluted with garbage, this definitely is not a dream.

Listen. Listen. Are you listening?!

Christina Bondi
Markham, ON Canada

Christina Bondi is currently a grade twelve high school student who resides in Markham, Ontario. Since she was a young girl, writing has always been a part of her life. Words are extremely powerful and play an important role in our society. Christina's dream is to one day become a poet or author. She thanks all of her family and friends for continuing to support her on this amazing journey.

Something for Everyone

He stayed awake one night and thought,
What's there for me, going to unfold?
Feels like I'm just here to rot
Feels like it's just getting old

Fear not, child, for it's not true
Don't think that your time is through
There is something there for you
Something waiting that is new

Still, he said, when times are tough
I think what I could have had
I think it's just not enough
Don't think it is all that bad

Something for everyone, something new
Waiting to unfold for you.

Rachel Marr
Broomfield, CO United States

This poem is based on the idea that everyone has something they're good at or someone they're important to. Everyone has to go through times when they don't have anything to do or anyone to talk to; but as someone with personal experiences, I believe there is something in life for everyone.

Home at Last

Lord, you looked down at her
and saw her suffering;
so you reached down,
smiled and took her hand.

She then looked up
and smiled back at you,
for she knew all her suffering
would soon be through.

Oh, the day she was laid to rest
she was in her mother's dress.
But, from us she didn't depart—
for she'll always live on in our hearts.

No, she did not say goodbye—
for when she finally did arrive,
She was greeted by loved ones
with their arms opened wide.

Though we may not know just when,
we will see her once again
on that day that God calls us home.

Vickey F. Romero
Corona, CA United States

To my mother, Virgie E. Hand. I was inspired by the Holy Spirit to write this poem for my loving ninety-four-year-old mother, after she went to her final home on July 2, 2012. She is forever in my heart.

Creatures of the Night

Are we creatures of the night
Do we have some secret
So dark that our soul's
Can't speak
Do we fear death

Is escape impossible
Are we trapped in a dark life
That centuries passes us by
But we never grow a day older
But centuries wiser

We feed on the blood of mortals
Us children of the dark
Frightening and extravagant
Mortals have hunted us
Fiercely and ambitiously
We have survived
In mortals hearts as legends
And fiction of their imagination.

Monique Lewin
Clarendon, Jamaica

My name is Monique Lewin from the small island nation Jamaica. Poetry has always been my love. When I do get the chance to write, it takes me to a place far away from this world. It gives a sense control how pen to paper makes me feel.

Personalities

Everyone is different
Life changes who you are
People come and go
Changing you forever
Each one leaving something different
Like a footprint on your heart
Teaching you a lesson
Making you strong each step of the way
Changing you every day
Showing kindness and love
Treating you like you're from above
Personalities change
But you are you either way
You start the day doing it your way
With friends, make the fun
That can never go way

Jessica Vollaro
Barrington, RI United States

My Star

My world is such an empty place,
And time goes on, at a slower pace.
My sweet memory, a gift from the past
To live in my heart, forever will last.

My grief and my pain, I still bear;
Many tears with others I share.
The sweetest voice, I hear anymore—
Your precious face, and the smile you wore.

We weathered life's storms together as one,
Walked hand in hand, toward the setting sun.
Beyond somewhere, your soul is there—
Resting in peace, no sorrow or cares.

When the stars light up Heaven so high,
I look up and wonder and silently cry...
Could that one that's shining so bright
Be my sweetheart, saying goodnight?

Lisa Gasswint
Abilene, KS United States

This poem was written by my dear grandma, who is now deceased. She wrote the poem shortly after my sweet grandpa, the love of her life, passed away. I am honoring her wishes by publishing her poems. My grandmother's name was Theora "Teddi" Brumbalow.

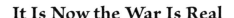
It Is Now the War Is Real

When the blood is finally on your hands,
when there is too much pain to feel.
When too many screams, just more demands..
It is now the war is real.

When the cries echo in your head,
when everything is too real...
when blue skies are blue black instead,
it is now the war is real.

When no one knows the end is near,
when no church bells are left to peal,
when there is no emotion left save fear...
it is now the war is real.

When all eyes and souls are hollow,
when there's no memory of a meal,
when there's no savior left to follow...
it is now the war is real.

Meryl C. Taylor
Conneaut, OH United States

So many of us do not realize the horror of life, until we are waist deep in it. This poem is dedicated to the suffering everywhere—whether the war is within or without. When we realize we all have blood on our hands, we all have our own battles with the world around us and within ourselves. My poem begs: Please realize we all suffer. Have compassion and understanding for the pain and suffering of those less fortunate. Do not wait for the war to be on our own doorstep; lend a hand, be positive, end the war. I thank my dear husband, Richard, and my friend and confidant, Dr. Todd Gates, for seeing me through my battles . It is with my words that I share the deepest wounds, the brightest hopes and the loftiest dreams that make me who I am.

Someday

Someday, I know I'll be there...
It takes time to reach a goal,
But I need to find a way deep within my soul.
To find happiness I searched so long for—
With a great heart and determination I wouldn't need more.

People say it takes a lot of courage to accomplish any dreams,
But I know this journey is like a river through many streams.
I will know when fate is there for me
Until I find happiness, then I will believe.

There is a dream that connects two different worlds.
A heavenly feeling flashed across the sky, I close my eyes.
Until someday, I know I'll be there...

My friends tell me it is far away where I am heading to.
Having their support comforts me, what I can do.
Others do not understand why I am doing this—
Deep in my heart, this chance I don't want to miss.

I worry myself, thinking this could be wrong;
But my heart tells me to stay strong.
Even far away places take time to find.
Believing hopes and dreams are on my mind.

If I don't make it, I won't give up or cry.
The revelation of my heart tells me I can try.
I am willing to search happiness without fear;
Even if the road is a long journey, I am strong to shed no tear.
Knowing that special someone is out there, somewhere—
Because I believe, someday, I know I'll be there...

Yen Ngan
Edmonton, AB Canada

Devin

The memories get hazy now as my mind and life move on
But I won't forget the day that we found out you were gone
I was only six years old without a worry in the air
I went to go watch television, maybe *Little Bear*
My mom came down, not long after, and she cried these dreadful tears
Swollen eyes, she drowned within them, stirring up my deepest fears
"What's going on?" I asked her, but she couldn't bare to say
I threw on my brown overalls as my heart sank away
I don't remember much from there or how I came to know
Did I cry, or was I in shock; where did my mind go?
Did I witness my father's curse to God, to his knees he would fall?
Did I see his arm pierce straight through that solid hallway wall?
Did I watch my mother's heart break when they said there was nothing
    they could do?
I know we must have all collapsed when we knew that it was true
The memories we shared together are near and dear to me
Although it feels I barely knew you, and this was all a dream
Oh, how different our lives would be if you were still around
Or even if we only knew the evil that brought you down
The days we had were limited; not knowing is the hardest part
It felt as if God personally reached in and tore out my heart
I see your picture, and I barely recognize you—no matter how I try
So what gives me the right to think of you and cry?
I guess that is the source of tears; it's the reason why I cry
Barely knowing who you were and how, now, I can never try.
I loved you then, and I love you now; forever in my heart, you'll be
I'll see you someday, baby brother, in the Land of Eternity.

Kelsi Cesarz
Burlington, WI United States

Born from Calamity

Pilgrims awashed ashore, fighting war after war
For life, love, and happiness, and liberty!

Against all odds we came, above reproach we rose.
Our banner being God above and Christ our abode!

'Tis our solemn oath and our divine decree
To shine in the darkness that all may be free!

Awaken posterity and hear the urgent call
Though darkness beckons us, we must not fall!

William Pittenger
Lawton, OK United States

Poetry is done on the fly for me, and it generally reflects my heart and soul concerning the state of war on morality, traditional values, and the United States Constitution, as well as the treachery, death, and unwarranted destruction of innocent lives. I produce when asked and after prayer, hoping that those who read my writing will be inspired to live better lives and heed the divine call to uphold the values of the Constitution, morality, and the higher ideals of the Holy Trinity as spoken of in the Bible.

Looking Out Your Window

When you are looking out your window
With your eyes fixed on the sky
Do you marvel or question
Do you feel the urge to cry?

Do you say a silent prayer
To the heavens, God above
Thanking Him for all His goodness
Tugging so close at your soul?

When you look outside your window
Do you rejoice in what you see?
All those tall trees reaching high
Trying to say "look at me"

Next time you are looking out your window
Try to focus and see
All the wonderful things
That God made for you and me.

Sara Aponte
Skokie, IL United States

I am Puerto Rican and was born to a family of twelve kids with eight girls and four boys. I am a wife to Luis Aponte, mother to two daughters, Zulma and Amanda, and mother-in-law of Jorje and Jonathan. I am also a grandmother to Jorje, Josiah, Alayah Jasara, Jenesis A'Marie and Janija Julissa. I enjoy writing, singing and teaching. I also do a lot of arts and crafts. I have a published book of poetry in Spanish, called De Mi para Ti , Poemas del Corazon. Most of my writing is in Spanish.

How Do I?

How do I tell you you're the love of my life
if you no longer believe in love?
How do I confess that when you look into my eyes
my heart stops and I lose my breath?
How do I prove I am different from the rest
when your mind tells you such a person doesn't exist?
How do I express my true feelings
when your heart is deaf and words have no meaning?
How do I say I want to grow old with you
when such a comment is frankly just old to you?
How do I proclaim your beauty captivates me
like the sun setting into a calm sea
or a warm breeze on a tropical beach?
How do I contain the youthful exuberance
that envelopes me in the presence of your elegance
and inspires me to write words that are so eloquent?
How do I prevent myself from loving you
when my soul quivers at the mere thought of you?
How do I find the way for you to understand
that soul mates do exist, and for every woman there is a man
who will stop at nothing to protect her, however he can?
How do I convince you, sometimes ignorance is bliss
but in turn, an opportunity for true happiness you may miss?
How do I articulate, that God made us cross paths—
that this is our destiny, our fate and our future is in his hands?

Luis Morales
Meriden, CT United States

I am Puerto Rican and live in Connecticut. I have always had a love for poetry since my early teenage years. This love for writing combined with my love of music made me realize I wanted to be a recording artist and songwriter. If it wasn't for my poetry, I would have never begun recording music with my group "La Comision" and been able to experience all the great things I have seen in my music career. Poetry was a way for me to express my feelings, thoughts and dreams in a private and personal way. I always kept my poetry to myself and barely shared it with anyone other than a few close friends. One of my friends, Zuleika, also loves poetry and always told me I was talented. One day, I went ahead and posted a couple poems on Poetry.com, and the feedback I received was incredible. I feel very humbled by this nomination and shocked to be mentioned with so many talented and gifted poets. This certainly certifies to me that writing, and poetry in particular, is a very important part of my life. I just hope my poems are able to connect with people and let them feel what I felt when I wrote them. Thank you to my family and friends for always supporting my endeavors and understanding that I am an artist and a dreamer.

Fly High, My Angel

Fly high, my angel
On the wings of the wind
Where I will join you
And see you again

On a beautiful day
When I will fall
When God decides
My ultimate call

We'll laugh and we'll play
On wings we will fly
For on that day
There's no reason to cry

We live to serve
And God will see
The rewards we deserve
Is what we achieve

Until that day
You will go where I go
In my heart you will stay
For I love you so

Kalei Sardinha
Waianae, HI United States

My life's dream is to win the Pulitzer for poetry. Most of my poems are based on real people and real life experiences. I am soon to be fifty-four years old, and I finally know what I want to do with my life! My poem was written for a very special angel—my Aunty Mary Ann, who journeyed to Heaven over a year ago. My soldier son, Zac, was away at army basic training in Virginia. Deeply saddened and unable to come home for our angel's farewell, I wrote this poem for my soldier, to let him know it was okay to mourn Aunty from afar.

The Colding

Gnarled branches, clutching, seeking any heat,
Stark-webbed across a grayling dawn;
What sky I saw was glacial summer gone
Reflecting only winter at its feet.
And nothing moved. Gray mice and moles beneath the snow
All huddled, grasping any warmth they could
To keep the virgin hearts alive. Throughout the wood
The hoary breath of chickadees hung low
Around the birds, like misty shields against the cold.
By noon, the day was old.

David Conary
Bryant Pond, ME United States

The Sound All Around

The world is a music box-like globe
Spinning the song of raindrops and snow
Bouncing off all of the things of the earth that grow
One sound for roses
One for trees
Its octave affected by their swaying in the breeze
And in fall when the leaves fall to the ground
the raindrops reveal the deepest symphonic sound
And in winter of cold, the notes strike a sharp;
The snowflakes will sound as light as a harp
And the music of spring and summer's day,
When the music is bold and great lights are on display
So come hear the music of the earth
Rekindle your passion, and feel your rebirth

Derek Walsh
Sherborn, MA United States

"M" for Strength

The sun shines through the window
like the hope in her eyes.
There's no feeling like it,
when she begins to smile.

People wonder what love brings—
if only they had spent
just one moment in her voice range.

With strength and fight in her bones,
no one knows the hope her heart forms
giving the ones she loves
the faith of never being alone.

Stubborn and tough through the days,
standing up for what she believes—
telling the world this is how it is
and that will never change.

Never too greedy, never too shy
arms reaching out to hold on tight,
always willing to help the ones who walk by;
a woman like this is hard to find.

Though a time will come,
no one will forget
the woman who taught us
the right way to live.

Keri Burke
New Paltz, NY United States

My poetry is my way of explaining who I am and what my emotions mean. There are never the right amount of words that can explain exactly what is running through my mind; yet a poem can always come from the ground up to try. I am not always thrilled with the way things I do turn out, except my poetry. I am always happy and thrilled with each poem I write. This is because I learned years ago, there's no right or wrong poem; it's what your heart believes. This is why I write, and this is why I feel.

Take Rise Against

when the time for change is near
your conscience seems to rise
passing thoughts now linger
with time, you realize
time at hand, the choice you make
are you to stand, are you to break?
Don't be scared, you will succeed
with a will, there is a way
your path you choose, your mind is made
don't give up, you will not fail

Robert Uttley
Sydney, NSW Australia

I'm just a normal guy expressing himself.

A Child's Hearse

The moon and stars dance in the sky,
As soldiers say their last goodbyes.
O, how the owl does sing his song,
As the aged young men march along.
They march towards the distant light,
As the booming guns pierce the night.
They reach the trenches one by one;
But suddenly, there's no more song.

My dear friends, please heed my warning:
All these wars we must be stopping.
The life we live is short and sweet,
But hate in the world, we must beat.
Or we'll welcome new life's first breath,
With an open casket, full of death.

Frederick Tamang
Camberley, Surrey United Kingdom

If I were to sum up my poetry in one word, it would be: me. All of my poetry reflects me as a person—my thoughts, my feelings and my opinions. It is very personal and all from the heart. Someone could easily read my personality and ideals just from glimpsing my poetry. I suppose my love for poetry was founded by the fact that I did not learn to write poetry from a teacher; rather, I learned this fine craft from the tip of Shakespeare's quill and Owen's shell-shocked trench.

The White Cat

Flat on his back, the white cat lies
Bum to the radiator, belly to the skies
Propriety-oblivious he's airing his drawers
But they're no more private than his four white paws.
Two black patches 'twixt two white ears
That turn to follow the sounds he hears.
A spot on his back and a long black tail
That undulates like a vapour trail.

His whiskers twitch and his mouth yawns wide
Displaying the rough, pink tongue inside.
It seems he's sleepy, but he's wide awake,
Monitoring the sounds that his family makes—
A fork on a dish or the rattle of a knife
Is all it takes to bring him to life.
Then he purrs and rubs with desire to be fed,
Kneads and stamps and butts with his head.

The reason I love him is hard to say:
He's his very own cat, in every way.
My home is his patch, he defends it well.
That we are his family is easy to tell,
But does he love me, or is it just good
That I come with comfort, kindness and food?

I know that I love him and hope that he
Experiences just as much pleasure from me.

Pat Sanderson
Doncaster, South Yorkshire United Kingdom

Grandma Went Back to Heaven

Grandma went back to Heaven, she only stayed a while
I knew she was an angel, ever since I was a child
There was Heaven in her touch, Heaven in her embrace
Kindness in her spirit, the love of God on her face
So peculiar were the words I'd hear Grandma say
"I must work the works of Him who sent me while it is day"
And work the works she did, all the way until her death
I believe she even praised the Lord with her last breath
She never wasted the opportunity to share the Gospel of truth
She'd say, "Do you know Him? You need to know Him, even in your
    youth"
I remember Grandma's cooking, everything was homemade
And helping her collect the eggs her chickens and geese had laid
I can picture her in her garden with her funny hat on
Tending carefully to her harvest, as she sang her favorite song
"Jesus on the main line, tell Him what you want
Jesus on the main line, tell Him what you want
Call Him up and tell Him what you want"
Even while she cooked, she would sing her songs
On TV *Little House on the Prairie* or *The Waltons* would be on
Everything that Grandma did, she did it God's way
The whole house could feel His spirit when she would kneel to pray
I thank God for a praying Grandma, for where would our families be?
I thank God for the prayer Grandma prayed for me
And when Grandma went back to Heaven, my heart felt the pain
But my soul rejoices in the fact that the gift of prayer remains
In everything Grandma said, and all that she did show
I know that where Grandma went, I will one day go

Jackie Moore
Colton, CA United States

Didn't Hear Your Call but Kept Safe in Your Arms

Far too many times, I heard you calling
But I didn't hear you call
You couldn't be visible to tell me
I was too far to be near you
I was only awaiting the time
The time I was visible
The only time to be near me
But flew up too high to listen
Only listening, I would know
Know that you would fall
If too near...you wouldn't let me
Because I've already missed the call
If I flew down you still wouldn't let me
I just couldn't take the answer
The answer of not knowing, not listening, not you around
Only because I wasn't around
If I didn't fly up you would've let me
But only because I was ashamed...just because
Because if I didn't know you...I wouldn't have a reason to fly up
But if I didn't fly up you wouldn't have caught me when I fell
Only falling would cure the heart
Because I would always know you would catch me
Catch me from the loneliness and into your arms
Only your arms would keep me safe
And I would always know
I would always know to keep coming back to you

Lizeth Hernandez
Los Angeles, CA United States

I'm a singer and a poet, so just call me a singing poet. Poetry is really the best way I get creative, but it's best when I put it in motion. It's the best way I delve into my feelings and stop focusing on my pain from Lupus. When I get into writing in different forms I love to write about love—because basically, it's a universal feeling anyone can understand. And I just adore the magical sense of love in life. When I become a singer, I just want people to understand it's from my heart. Don't underestimate me.

Lover's Poem

I wanted to write a lover's poem—with lover's dreams, and lover things.
But how can I write a lover's poem, when I myself I'm not yet grown,
And have no lover to call my own?
How could I know a lover's heart?
How I can a see a lover's dream,
Or know of lover things?
Where should I go, if I want to know of all these lover things?
Perhaps it is a lesson learned in time, forged with broken hearts;
But then again, who am I to question a lover's heart?
I wanted to write a lover's poem—perhaps I will one day, when I am
    grown.
Perhaps I'll have a lover and lover's dreams and lover things.
Until that day, I will say:
One day, I'll write a lover's poem.

Kristine Miller
Clarkston, MI United States

Ricky's Poem

The souls you touched and the many hearts you would win
With that straightforward smile or your silly little grin
Your voice, your laugh, was music to our ears
Now the silence is sometimes too hard to bare
The time we had just wasn't enough
Yes, it's hard trying to be tough
You weren't eighty, nor thirty, but a mere eleven years
The hurt, the tears, when forced to face our fears
It was far from right, it was definitely not fair
No new memories we can share
Selfish were we, to want and need you here
Why did God have to take you up there?
As days, weeks, months, and even years will pass by
The pain will remain, deep inside
No more I love yous or kisses we fright
Never again can we hug you goodnight
No one can tell what their future brings
One thing is certain: God gave you wings
Ricky, our little man, the Lord's angel above
We pray you know how deeply you're loved
One day we'll all be together again
The day we will no longer live in sin
No one knows when that day will come
The day our family is reunited with our son, brother, and little man
The day our eternal life begins

Kiya McDonnold
Sikeston, MO United States

A Gift from God

Sisters are a gift from God
Believe me, I know what I say
A brother for me was not meant to be
But sisters, I've got three!

It is great to have several sibs
You teach and learn from them
Whether you are close or not
That alone can contribute a lot!

Sisters are a joy to have
You love them from your heart
Sharing peace at play and at rest
And you hope for them all the best!

The best of love, life and happiness
And healthy lives will be theirs
I pray to God for them each day
And will make it known in my own special way!

Saundra Russell
Tucson, AZ United States

Ms. Saundra Russell has been writing poetry for at least fifty years. She is a health care professional and obtained a master's degree from New York University. She lives with her husband, and her interests include integrative medicine (eastern and western), crafting, writing poetry and traveling. (She has traveled to five continents thus far.) She does volunteer work in the community focusing on various health and veteran issues...where the inspiration for her poetry begins!

Me, My Love, and Our Secret

Not broken, just broken-hearted
Over the secret that is my life
The truth is what's hurting me
Turning me into a shell
Of one big secret
Threatening to split my life in two
I can't say it
Can't even think of it
In the light I chose
I must keep his secret
Or I'll lose more than myself
Who I am is nothing aside from him
And who I am is his secret too
But why does it not haunt him?

Ashley Williams
Manassas, VA United States

I've been in love with poetry since I could read. I greatly appreciate the emphasis my mother put on the literary aspect of my education. My fiancé and I both have a passion for poetry and pray to pass it on to any children we have in the near future. I am thrilled about publishing for the first time, so the world can perhaps share my passion with me and help me grow as a writer.

All Broken Records Have That Familiar Scratching Sound

The words fumble out of your mouth
So awkwardly,
As if you didn't mean to say them.

That every hesitant syllable
And over-thought inflection
Was just an attempt to persuade
My mind of something
You refused to admit.

And we said there'd be a forever,
An infinite love.
But we're both smart enough to know
That perpetual motion doesn't exist,
That love cannot be created or destroyed—
Just transferred.

So I'll listen to your broken thoughts
And hollow concepts,
Knowing that their meaning
Has nothing to do with
Your intentions.

But go on,
I don't mean to interrupt.
Its just hard for me to swallow the fragments
Of my heart and your b*llsh*t.
So forgive me if I can't focus on
Your practiced monologue.

Johnathon Peters
San Antonio, TX United States

It started off as a coping mechanism, a way to explain the experiences of my chronic loneliness; but God had other plans for it, better plans for me. This is nowhere near my best work, but it's all significant and sentimental to me. I'm a work in progress, just like my poetry.

Walk Up the Slide

future science fiction puzzle
muzzles constant conscious thought
of children sneezing
while wasting petals in the wind
while choking on plants
undoing grass like cheese-string
needles for sewing the earth to the ocean
fitting fabric in a camel sore's eye sore
building a Legoland jungle near the sun
and dreaming Awake Away
a land in field of evergreen
a lad on top of knolls in Ireland
Scotland, picking daises

(and walking up the wrong side of slides)

Liza Meyers
Rego Park, NY United States

A New American

You came here to America
So young...from far away...
Your hopes and dreams lived in your heart
Each and every day.

You shared your talents in this land...
Everything so strange and new.
You embraced a different lifestyle
And saw your dreams come true.

Grateful for opportunities
This country did provide.
Today, you're a U.S. citizen
And filled with love and pride.

America's very grateful
For immigrants like you who see...
And bring so much to share with all
In this great Land of the free!

Patricia J. Mack
Livonia, MI United States

Poetry has always and continues to help me express and recall the most meaningful experiences in my life. This particular poem was born out of my very special friendships with immigrants who appreciate and value America—sometimes more than its natural citizens do. Many Americans too often take our land of freedom for granted. We should all be ever-mindful of those who sacrificed their lives defending the freedom we all enjoy. Freedom is a God-given gift that Americans should willingly share with those who come from foreign lands genuinely seeking it.

Ageless Flow

Between close friends
Commiserating, sharing
Things said and unsaid.
The way it is, you know.

An ageless flow
Between close friends.
No need to pretend.
No need to hide anything.
A trust, a bond
Regard and respect
Always present—
Being in the flow, you know.

An ageless flow
Between close friends.
Kidding, joking
Laughing and crying;
Reflecting on life's
Highs and lows with
With honesty of heart
Integrity of soul.
Always there, you know
Timeless, seamless our flow.

An ageless flow
Between close friends,
Me and Joe.

Dale O. McCoy
Denver, CO United States

My Life Story

There were tears on my face, when I could not run in the life's fast race.
I was only left behind because the bird of time I could not bind.
Today, I feel that I was wrong,
The time always gave me a gong,
My conscience tried to complain, but it was already too late.
I used to curse my luck at first,
But soon my face was in dirt.
For it was my luck which always helped,
But I never woke up instead.
At last my ambition was destroyed,
And I was drowned in my own sweat—
But it was the wrong time to feel sorry for me,
As the time had already defeated me.
Then the day came when I was dead,
And, of course! My grave was prepared.
People gave their children my example,
So that time they do not trample.
Now I realized my position,
But I was in a terrible situation.
Sitting in my grave today I feel,
Work and work was the only means.
Anyway my life was finished,
I could not do whatever I wished.
Oh dear! On my grave it was carved:
"Walk with time, else you will starve."

Nidhi Bhatia
Calgary, AB Canada

The Real Fairy Tale

Everything starts perfect—
as a child, you feel
blessed, and you're living the best story.

As time goes,
you start to stumble;
you find yourself...lost.

The real fairy tale
is in your soul and heart;
broken dreams can end.
Like Heaven's door
you never know
what the future
has to offer.

The story changes all the time.
Nothing is impossible
so live your nightmare—
or find your rose garden.

Anna Nickolausson
Almhult, Kronoberg Sweden

Since early childhood, I have always had a great imagination; my writing began when I was ten years old. When I write, I feel I get it all out so much more. I feel I'm reaching out more and can make others think twice. I take my writing as a gift—and when you have a gift, you should use it to help others. I know I do that at the same time when I write. Being able to feel better and give others something at the same time makes me feel like a better person.

Natural Herbs

As the days go by and life goes on,
The struggles are getting harder;
Doctors work all day trying to save lives
Yet, we are dying faster.

There are many cures out there, I know,
But the scientist still need to see
That the natural herbs are the only cure
To be prescribed for you and me.

The elderly are the ones to ask—
They know the herbs we need.
Eat all the foods we grow ourselves,
And use most of the flower seed.

Pamela Forde
Bridgetown, Barbados United States

Believer

Ever since I was a child,
Unyielding thoughts inside me glided;
Those rooted beliefs on which I thrive
Render me the vital drive.

Built not of bricks and sands,
But of grandparents with caressing hands;
Weaving irrevocable love's invisible strands
Through my blood and flesh-filled lands.

Whatever I believe in would surround
Conspiring everything in the world around—
With the much awaited answers found
A divine upheaval in my heart's mound!

There settles in a restless peace
To put my fellow beings at ease.
Those awakening dreams never cease;
The burning spirit within me, they unleash.

How a raindrop in an oasis would see
The thirst of millions set free!
I wish to take this compassionate spree
Inspired by the believer in me!

Madhini Maran
Singapore, Republic of Singapore

As the poem suggests, I have always been a deep-rooted believer in all that I do. Thanks to my parents and brother, for firmly believing in my capabilities. As a chemical engineer by profession, poetry has been a stress reliever to me. It is equivalent to transcendental meditation; it streamlines my thoughts and allows me to travel within myself. It gives me a clarity of mind, which is reflected in the form of my poems.

I Lost a Friend Today

Joy filled my soul two weeks ago, when to my door you came
To once again renew our lifelong friendship bond
How long since last I saw you—one year, maybe two

Across our lives it's been that way, time would come and go
A day, a month, one year, with only a letter or maybe two
But it seemed like only yesterday—our bond still grew and grew

We sat and talked and reminisced of things we used to do
Adventures lived, excitement felt from life's long passing parade
Memories shared of days gone by—we were a pair, we two

Too soon that day came to a close, you struggled up to leave
With age, slowed step and dimming eyes, you shuffled toward the door
My lifelong pal, my dearest friend—so old, so loyal and true

That fateful morning came the call, I scarce could believe my ears
"Dad's joined the sunset" said the voice, you are the first to know
The shock set in, my tears ran free—why you? Why not me?

And now I stand on hilltop high, just the wind your ashes and me
I gaze out to the spot we loved, where we so often came
With shaking hands and empty heart—in the wind, I set you free

Arthur Harwood
Cowley, AB Canada

This poem is to commemorate a friendship that spanned more than sixty-five years. As children, we grew up next door to one another, where the bond began. Our friendship continued through youth, young adulthood and then through our mature years, and finally into old age; it was one of those special friendships where a year or more would slip by without us seeing one another, but when we did, it seemed as if our last visit was only yesterday. He came to see me one last time. Two weeks later, he passed away in his sleep. I write this for all who have lost lifelong friends and/or spouses.

For You

Young we were when I first felt it
Opening myself to you
Underestimating the challenges we would both go through

Silently festered
The seed of doubt
Incessantly plotting
Leaving me weak
Living out its bitter lie

Hollow I felt when we fell through
Alone in my thoughts
Valiantly trying to make things right
Everything seemed too scrambled to be the truth

Moments pass by and they don't feel right.
You're the missing piece to my life.

Happiness stands a lifetime away
Eternity I'll wait if I have to
All just to hold you
Returning it all back to reality
To just let you know that I love you

Anthony Cole
Fort Bragg, NC United States

Writing in general has always been a very big part of my life—from writing notes to writing a novel. To me, it matters not what you write about, as long as you never regret it. I am proud to serve in the U.S. Army, and I hope my writing helps someone in life.

A Birthday Wish for My Best Friend

I know my card is running late—
Another year, it must be fate.

No matter how hard I try,
My plans seem to go awry.

Just once I'd love to get it right
And make your special day shine bright.

If I could grant your fondest wish,
I'd serve it on a golden dish.

If a genie I could command,
I'd have him grant your every demand.

There are no riches to compare
With the friendship that we share.

When your problems seem too tall,
All you need to do is call.

Though I have moved far away,
In my heart you'll always stay.

So though your day has come and gone,
Rest assured our friendship is going strong.

And because to me you are very dear,
I'm wishing you a wonderful "Birthday Year!"

Mary Lindsay
Peach Springs, AZ United States

True Beauty

They make you feel that you are ugly
But deep inside, you are really fine.
What you need to do is put opinions of others aside
And go ahead and walk that beautiful line.

They talk about your weight and call you fat;
But look inside and you will find
A beautiful girl bursting out,
And a beautiful body working out.

You are fine just the way you are
Just look at yourself from the inside-out
And you will find
That outside beauty is not everything.

If you think it is,
Don't you worry—
God knows where your true beauty lies.

Jennifer SkyAnne Storey
Carrollton, MS United States

Reckless Indifference

The night is calming
Impressing a forever chill within my soul
Forgotten faces whispering yesterday's goodbyes
Broken thoughts piecing together a future that will never be whole

Pondering life's journey
Escaping the future for an imprisoned past
Marching into a blank abyss
Vigilante, I walk through valleys of doubt for an answer
to a question that will never be found
Not even a flicker of light to guide my senses
Erasing footsteps to everything I have ever known
Empty echoes screaming for a name
A name to an author to the story that will never be told

Michael Wright
Princeton, ME United States

My poetry derives not from what my mind is thinking, but what my soul is feeling. It is rather a release of inhibition. I see writing as I see life: as a beautiful introspect into the raw workings of the universe. I have written speeches for various public officials and also work in law. My writings also expand into songwriting and fiction.

You're the One

You're the one I really love
You're the one I wanna kiss
You're the one who owns my heart
You're the one I really miss
You're the one who I think of all day
You're the one I dream about
You're the one that's in my head
And will not stay out
You know I really love you
And I wanna make you mine
And it kills me that you aren't here tonight
You know there's something I wanna say
But I just can't spit it out
My tears will tell you all the things I keep in my head
That my mouth can't say at all
The bond is getting stronger the moment you're away
It makes me wanna see you more everyday
But it also makes me miss you, it also makes me cry
I wanna see your smiling face every time I wanna die
Just one more thing before I have to go
You're everything I need, you're everything I want

Caitlyn Whitten
Ames, OK United States

Saving Grace

I can hear my heart breaking
every single time
I gaze upon this beautiful girl—
Wrapped in ribbons of shadows dancing,
Lost in a shiny spinning razor wire world.
Even as all the glitz and glamour smile
upon her, it cannot make her whole.
Seduced by a smoldering secret blue void
with an incredibly ravenous hold.
Her hunger and her fear—equally insatiable—
keeping her entombed in writhing cold.
Smoke and mirrors masking all,
Including roads that lead to heart and home.
Unaware of the rapture that is hers to take
in place of the wounds that she presently owns.
This song of love and light, I give her
in hopes it will console
Find within your heart forgiveness;
this saves even the most tortured of souls.
Listen to my heart breaking,
Maybe then you'll know.

Carmelita Gallo
Barrigada, GU Guam

Me and You

You stuck by me when times got tough
You held my hand when I felt like giving up
You could make me laugh when I wanted to cry
And you held me close when I wanted to die
You've taught me a lot about love and life
You gave me my family and made me your wife
You never gave up on me when I felt like giving in
You are more than my lover—you are my best friend
I thank God every night that he brought us together
And together we can make it through any kind of weather
We've had our ups and downs, like all in love do
But we've become stronger for that, me and you
No matter what happens, we'll be together still
I love you, Daniel, and I always will

Amanda Cadwallader
Cherry, IL United States

Our Dark Judgments

Encompassed in the dank of July eve
With pregnancy my brain seems to employ
Of how, so curt, love's brevity ensued
to wait upon the wither of her joy.

'Tis fabulous—the plots that darkness weaves
When mingled with memories and paraffin
Where only sweet and sweetness come to mind
And holds its passion, time and time again.

I, lost within his hand, could see no star
A canopy of blades deprived my eye
But willing, I went forth with guided feet
Yoked to a swain whose valor held the sky.

And in this dance, reliance I did hold
As he in her for what has yet to be
Unconfident of judgments left unspoken
Left waiting in the dank for only she.

So while this dejection faintly holds my core
Still shooting Cupid's arrows straight and true
Know that if relinquished, you become
There's still a flame tonight in eyes of blue.

Andrea Dana
Morrice, MI United States

For Shari

Lash me to the mast
that I may hear
the siren song of the sea

When Midas' dawn
sets the waves aglow
and whips wind to blow
from crest to crest
wild salt spray

to drench!

To drench!

O, the thirst to quench!
Of those who would know
the siren song of the sea.

Tim Pike
Fossil, OR United States

Love's Music

You played me
Blue strings extending straight to my veins
Fluting notes scattered like freckles
Butterflies murmur in stomach drums
A symphony of tingles when we kiss
I sway to your heartbeat's rhythm
Deft notes whisper a sweet duet
Your voice, a coffee-colored cello's song
Lute strings brushed like eyelashes softly closing
Fingers running over skin like piano keys
Hum of contentment rising out of a golden, brass chest
The music of loving you

Sasha Kasoff
Tomales, CA United States

I have wanted to be a teacher since first grade. I started writing my poems down in sixth grade, and I started my lesson plans when I was a freshman in high school. I have written hundreds of poems, a handful of songs, and am currently working on a fantasy novel. My name, Sasha, means protector and defender of mankind— which I try to live up to. I want to teach in the hopes of infecting others with my love for words. Find time to be creative and rekindle your love of learning: read, laugh, collage, hike, and be merry.

American Football

"It doesn't matter if you win or lose,
It's how you play the game!"
Losers' talk! Hitting and getting hit
It's a passionate game; Blood, grit, pain
A sense of accomplishment, teamwork, toughness
Rewards are in the strive
Passing and running, interceptions and fumbles
A lot of junk-talking and sweating while the stadium rumbles
Rewards are in the strive
Pushing and blocking; each has his mission
Executing best-laid plans from HQs, strategic battles of attrition
Some teams are just deeper and better
Rewards are in the strive
Big dudes, little dudes, fast dudes and slow dudes
Eleven per side. One says, go: the other says, no
Advancing and pushing, resisting and tackling
Each avoiding yellow flags, backing
Rewards are in the strive
But when the big strive does not yield and efforts came up short
There are team regrets. Team goals have not been met. Individual
    failures
Rewards were in the strive
Now it's over
But when the big strive does yield and the crowds rush the fields
When the final whistle blows and everybody's jumping on their toes
The rewards from the strive are topped by the prize!
And the Champion is...

Lindsey Ham
Goldsboro, NC United States

*I am a modern-day Renaissance man. I have been wonderfully blessed by God
with many different professional abilities and talents. One of them is writing
poetry. This is an awesome ability to have when you're a "Renaissance man"
with a type-A personality in a great athlete's body! I have been able to write
poetry as I was experiencing this absolutely action-packed, exciting life, and the
result is a poetic history of some of my experiences.....a literal library of beautiful,
interesting, revealing, emotionally intellectual yet spiritually grounded stuff.*

Somebody

I am somebody who changes every minute
Somebody no one can handle
Somebody who can laugh on the outside while crying on the inside
Somebody who can put on a blank face and be strong
or can be broken by a single insult
Somebody who has been beat into the ground too many times
but still stands strong every day at school
one who is always judged
because no one sees behind the mask
I am somebody who hates herself
but cares for others
Somebody who smiles in the morning
and cries at night
I am this somebody

Jessica Rodrigues
State Center, IA United States

I am eighteen years old and going to college for nursing. I started writing in the eighth grade to help me cope with life's issues. My poetry is influenced by my life experiences. With my mom and stepdad's love and support, I will continue to write. I have been told that some of my poetry is kind of dark. But I write what I feel at the moment. I am a shy person who puts all of my emotion in my writing. I would like to thank my family and my fiancé for all their love and support. Thank you.

Love Is Forever

Do you know how I feel about you?
Of course you don't; I never had the courage to say.
What should I do?
I can't help but think of you every day
You mean more to me than my own life
I have always loved you for who you are
Why couldn't you have just said, "Will you be my wife?"
A toast to you, my love—alone, I sip the champagne at the bar
All I have ever wanted was for you to think of me
I hope that we will meet again in Heaven
Whenever that may be
We will embrace each other at the stroke of eleven
I am sorry, my love, but with my last breath…
I will say "I love you," before my untimely death

Jazmine Jade Soule
Aurelia, IA United States

As an aspiring author, I have always loved all kinds of writing. To me, poetry isn't about making sentences rhyme, but about developing character and expressing feelings. My parents have always told me if you find something that you are passionate about, stick with it and you will make something with yourself. This is what I have always believed in. My life has been wonderful, and I have become a success at a young age.

Stuff

Everywhere in my house, there's stuff
It's in every nook and cranny
Some of it I bought my own self
Some handed down from my granny

And if you look in my yard, more stuff
Can't blame anyone else but me
For some reason, I thought 'twas needed
And so it was purchased by me

Well, finally I have enough stuff
It's taken over all of my space
Can't find room for necessities now
Stuff is staring me in the face

Guess it's time now for a yard sale
Or maybe donate to the thrift store
For, if I don't get rid of some stuff now
How can I ever find room for some more?

Alyce Green
Indian Valley, ID United States

I am a great-great-grandmother in my early seventies. I have written nonsensical poetry for many years, and it was never intended to be great poetry. I have written a few more serious ones; still, just do it for fun. I am retired, and my hobby is reading...a lot.

Trying to Get By

I pick out my clothes for the day
Remind myself not to care what people say
Throw my hair in a bun
Hoping I'll have some fun
A small confident voice speaks to me
But my insecurities are louder times three
These feelings of loneliness and abandonment I feel
I'm haunted by myself and wish this wasn't real
But my luck turns to be sour
And the clock rings another hour
I can't shake the feelings from my shoulders
My wounded heart slowly grows colder
I try to build a wall
It gets tough to keep standing tall
My eyes sting and flare with hate
As the first pathetic tears overtake
I just want to throw my phone away
No one cares to call or text a simple "hey"
My expression hardens and I give a cold laugh
"Like I care," I think and wish to unleash my wrath
But I know that would be wrong
So I push my way through the throng
I keep walking down the hall with a sigh
Knowing I'll struggle, just trying to get by

Alina Brown-Smith
Kingston, WA United States

Fourth of July, Standing Knee-Deep in History

Evening fall and voices call
On history's golden string!
My heart is breathless standing still
While muted silence sings!

Of great heroic, golden deeds,
Of courage strong and brave
Persistent, persevering wills...
The love they freely gave!

But most of all, a tenderness
Is carved from every name
On twilight's sweetest music, from
Our history's Hall of Fame.

God bless America!

Dan Flewelling
Ponca City, OK United States

Have Faith In Me, for I Am God

My wings flutter in the morning air
As the children dance about in the annual fair
Far away, the devotees kneel in prayer to their Lord
Have faith in me, for I am God

I am born a Hindu, a Muslim, a Christian, a Jew
I am loved, neglected, abandoned, killed
I live in a palace, an orphanage, a room for few
Or on the streets, where my blood is spilled

I chant the holy mantras in Lord Shiva's temple
I kneel in prayer in Jesus's Church
My heart beats to Allah's chord
Have faith in Me, for I am God

I murder the Muslim before me, wearing the cloak of the devil
I slaughter the Hindu, the plunderer, the epitome of evil
I vanquish the Jew, for he is a menace, the unwanted pest
I destroy the Christian, for my faith is always above the rest

Night has fallen as I awake, shaking off the war lust
My hands are bloody, but in God we trust
Tears course down my face, as I regard his broken form
But alas, there's no time for regret, as hatred is the norm

I am in the victor, in the vanquished, in the murderer and the
     murdered
I am in man, and omnipresent, in the many burdens he has shouldered
I becalm him, I resurrect him, I remove his fear
I instill in him the essence of humanity, as I whisper in his ear
"Have faith in Me, for I am God"

Chirag Subramanian
Manipal, Karnataka India

The Riddle

Starless night of clear, black skies
Awaits the day of war
Fate controls the winner's loss
And awards the losers more

Crystal eyes of many colors
Foresee the truth at hand
Prophetess of love and hate
Who's unknown across our land

And even though she may possess
A power greater than me
It's hidden from her human eyes
The greatness she can see

To make the blind become uncovered
Is the mystery for you
But before I leave, I have to say
I've given you a clue.

Rebecca Rieder
Germantown, WI United States

I am currently a full-time student in Wisconsin. I love writing, and I made it my goal my freshman year of high school to be a published poet within five years. It's extremely surreal to have achieved this goal. I hope everyone that reads my poem sincerely enjoy it, because I know I enjoyed writing it for you.

A Key 'Round Her Neck

The daughter that was left to her own defenses
wearing only a key 'round her neck
that offered no comfort or protection
The parents now with death at their door, their shame now
commences
To the family who turned a blind eye and was never there
only to point a finger of blame to hide their own shame
The daughter turned mother gave her soul and more
to the children she bore
She could never fill the hole of her empty childhood
the mother-still-daughter wandering with her key
longing for the parents that never could be

Sonja Timmermans
Moordrecht, ZH Netherlands

I was born in Nottingham, England in the year of '78 on Valentine's Day. My family, like some of yours out there, was/is very dysfunctional. My youth was a very sad and confusing one; a lot of my inspiration comes from my past experiences. I was never blessed with outstanding talents, brains or beauty—however, I feel my undiscovered talent does lie in my poetry. I now live a happier life with my husband and darling daughter in Holland. My experiences now gained are of a happier and peaceful nature. Please read and enjoy my work.

Index

CPSIA information can be obtained at www.ICGtesting.com
Printed in the USA
BVOW031746051112

304580BV00002B/5/P